I0064036

UNDERSTANDING THE BLACK ECONOMY AND
BLACK MONEY IN INDIA

ALSO BY ARUN KUMAR

The Black Economy in India
Indian Economy Since Independence:
Persisting Colonial Disruption
Challenges Facing Indian Universities (Edited)

UNDERSTANDING THE BLACK ECONOMY AND BLACK MONEY IN INDIA

AN ENQUIRY INTO CAUSES, CONSEQUENCES AND REMEDIES

ARUN KUMAR

ALEPH

This is a Print On Demand copy and hence does not have special finishing on the cover.

ALEPH

ALEPH BOOK COMPANY
An independent publishing firm
promoted by *Rupa Publications India*

First published in India in 2017
by Aleph Book Company
7/16 Ansari Road, Daryaganj
New Delhi 110 002

Copyright © Arun Kumar 2017

The author has asserted his moral rights.

All rights reserved.

The views and opinions expressed in this book
are the author's own and the facts are as reported
by him, which have been verified to the extent
possible, and the publishers are not in any way
liable for the same.

No part of this publication may be reproduced,
transmitted, or stored in a retrieval system, in any
form or by any means, without permission in
writing from Aleph Book Company.

ISBN: 978-93-86021-57-1

1 3 5 7 9 10 8 6 4 2

This book is sold subject to the condition that it
shall not, by way of trade or otherwise, be lent,
resold, hired out, or otherwise circulated without
the publisher's prior consent in any form of
binding or cover other than that in which it is
published.

For Neerja, my wife, for being there…which helped me understand this subject like nothing else could have

CONTENTS

INTRODUCTION

....~...

The sudden announcement by Prime Minister Narendra Modi on 8 November 2016 that ₹500 and ₹1,000 notes would no longer be legal tender subjected hundreds of millions of Indians, especially the poorest of the poor, to unnecessary distress. Hundreds of thousands of daily wage earners, shopkeepers and small traders lost their livelihoods, and the country's economy suffered a major setback. In the weeks that followed, it soon became apparent that the Prime Minister's initiative had not been properly thought through and, worse, was ineffectually implemented. While the mid-term and long-term effects will take time to manifest themselves, there is little doubt in my mind that demonetization should not have been imposed on the country. We will look at what went wrong in greater detail later on in the book. Suffice it to say that the demonetization has had little effect on the problem of the black economy. The irony, of course, is that the reason for the exercise cannot be faulted, for the black economy is the main reason why India continues to be a poor, underprivileged country, all the economic gains of the past few decades notwithstanding.

India's black economy is estimated to be 62 per cent of GDP—generating (at 2016-2017 prices) about ₹93 lakh crore of revenue (or $1.4 trillion). It is larger than the income generated by agriculture and industry put together, which is about 39 per cent of GDP. It is larger than the size of government (centre plus states) spending, which is about 27 per cent of GDP. Because of its existence, the country's economy has been losing on an average 5 per cent growth (when compared to official figures) since the mid-1970s when the black economy became significant. If we add 5 per cent to the rate of growth over the past four decades or so, the size of our economy would be ₹1,050 lakh crore (or about $15 trillion at the current rate of exchange) instead of ₹150 lakh crore (or $2.2 trillion) as it is now. We would have become the world's second largest economy, behind the US, and a middle-income nation. The per capita income of the country would have been ₹7.4 lakh (or $11,000) instead of about ₹1 lakh or ($1,500) as it is at present. In other words, every one of us would have been seven times richer on average.

In the course of this book, we will see how and why the black economy thrives in India, how it holds us back from achieving our potential, where it began, why initiatives like the demonetization of currency do not put a dent in it, and what sort of remedies should be undertaken in the short, medium and long term to root it out.

The book is organized in the following way. Chapter I presents an analysis of what the black economy is. People think it only has to do with unaccounted income. Others see it as a parallel economy. Those in the West think of it as an informal sector of the economy, which is only true of the advanced countries. This chapter explains why the black economy in developing countries is different from that seen in the advanced economies. This clarity is needed if it has to be measured, its consequences discussed, and remedies proposed.

Chapter II discusses the reasons why the black economy is bad for India. This chapter looks at the macro- and micro-economic effects of the black economy.

Chapter III looks at the specifics of the black economy's effect on government and civil society.

Chapter IV looks at the underlying causes of the black economy. It goes deep into the various misconceptions about the phenomenon and discusses its origins and historical context.

Chapter V discusses the various steps the government has taken over the past seventy years, including the ill-advised demonetization of currency in 2016. It examines the various suggestions and recommendations made by numerous committees and commissions that have analysed the situation. Despite everything that has been proposed and tried, the black economy has only grown, proving that the causes have not been correctly identified nor the right remedial actions taken.

In conclusion, I've made the point that there is no magic wand to do away with the black economy in this country. It needs carefully thought through remedies, not populist measures, incorruptible governments with the political will to act and the patience to keep implementing strategies in the mid- and long-term. Only then will India be able to unlock its real potential.

◆

The last time the black economy occupied everyone's attention before the 2016 demonetization was in 2011 when a succession of scams surfaced and Anna Hazare and Arvind Kejriwal spearheaded a movement to root out corruption in the country. Another movement with the same objective was subsequently led by Baba Ramdev. In the 2014 general election this issue became central, with the BJP promising to bring back the black money held abroad by wealthy, corrupt Indians. The party's leaders promised that when all this money was brought back, every Indian family would be ₹15 lakh richer. That has not happened, nor has there been any cessation in the growth of the black economy.

Government Steps to Curb the Black Economy

Since coming to power in 2014, the NDA government has tried various steps to tackle the black economy. Among them are the Black Money (Undisclosed Foreign Income and Assets) and Imposition of Tax Act, 2015; Gold Monetization Scheme, 2015; Income Declaration Scheme (IDS), 2016; Benami Transactions (Prohibition) Amendment Act, 2016, and so on. Despite all this, it has not had much success in dismantling the black economy. We will see later in the book why the efforts of the NDA government, and the governments that have preceded it, have met with extremely limited success.

As I have said, and as I will demonstrate later in the book, the fundamental reason why no government has been able to solve the problem is because the black economy and its causes and effects have not been properly understood. This lack of understanding has meant that even well-meaning efforts to tackle it have failed. The situation that has prevailed, and that continues to prevail, is rather like the parable of the seven blind men and the elephant. One touches the tail and thinks it is a broom, another touches the trunk and thinks it is a hose-pipe, a third touches the legs and thinks they are the pillars of a building. Similarly, various governments, their advisers and civil society leaders have looked at various aspects of the problem, without quite getting to grips with the whole. For instance, a legal committee might think changing the laws would address the problem; NGOs might advocate greater expenditures on essentials, like education; economists might suggest a change in economic policies; and a technology person may suggest use of technology—the general public views all these efforts with cynicism since nothing tried by the government has delivered as yet.

Misconceptions About the Black Economy

I will go deeper into the misconceptions about the black economy later on in the book, but I think it would be useful to dispel some basic fallacies right at the outset. People often think of the black economy and corruption as being synonymous. That is not the case. Corruption involves a quid pro quo either in cash or in kind. In other words, if I do a special favour to someone they would then give me a bribe in cash or kind. But in much of the black economy there may be no quid pro quo.

I could give tuitions and earn an income that I do not declare to the tax authorities. As a trader I could resort to under-invoicing to earn an extra income but I do not give a bribe for that. No quid pro quo is involved in these and many other activities. While there is illegality in not declaring the black income that has accrued, this is not corruption as it is generally understood.

Thus, black income generation and corruption are not synonymous. However, they do have a two-way relationship. As corruption increases so does the size of the black economy and vice versa. The increase in corruption correlates well with independent estimates that the size of the black economy is growing.

Very often it is thought that the black economy is a phenomenon solely concerning the public sector. However, it has been shown that the black economy is a joint product of the public and private sectors. In fact, it may be argued that its magnitude is larger in the private sector than the public sector.

Some argue that the black economy does not matter since it is a part of one and the same economy along with the white economy and, therefore, results in higher levels of output and employment. For example, lawyers not disclosing their full income spend on travel, entertainment and other things out of the extra income. In addition, they create employment and their work creates additional output. If India has a black economy in addition to its white economy, the natural implication is that the country's actual economy is much larger than the official figure. So, if the black economy is 62 per cent of GDP in 2016-2017, then the actual economy instead of being ₹150 lakh crore would be ₹243 lakh crore. Isn't that something to celebrate? Shouldn't we be happy that the country is more prosperous than official data reveals?

The fallacy in this argument is that the economic potential of the nation is actually lowered by the black economy rather than being enhanced. For instance, if roads are made with an inadequate amount of tar to bind the aggregates so as to make money they will soon be damaged by rainfall. So, instead of making new roads (of which there is a huge deficit), we keep repairing the same roads every six months. The potholed roads slow traffic down and lead to increased wear and tear of vehicles, all of which negatively impacts productivity.

The black economy is one of the biggest reasons for the failure of state policies—the result of which is that society is unable to achieve its goals. It sets back development. And so it follows that the larger the black economy, the greater its negative impact on the economy.

There is an assumption that is made by some analysts that checking the black economy would be a zero sum game with resources being redistributed from one part of the economy to the other. It is argued that one part of the economy will simply be converted into the other without any additional gain. However, this is not true and the elimination of the black economy would be a positive sum game with those adversely affected by the elimination also benefiting. If the economy were to be seven times larger today, the businessmen presently generating black incomes would also be at least seven times richer in spite of paying more taxes.

Is All The Black Money Abroad?

Yet another popular misconception is that most of the black money generated by the black economy is lying abroad in foreign bank accounts, mainly in Swiss banks. Certainly through the flight of capital the rich and powerful have been moving funds to tax havens. However, as there has been no comprehensive official study of how much black money is stashed away abroad, we must look to other sources for whatever confirmation is to be had. According to a study, the opportunity cost of the flight of capital for the Indian economy was ₹135 lakh crore (or $2 trillion) between 1948 and 2012. Broadly speaking, it is the opportunity that the economy is missing. So, it is the amount that is taken out of the country along with the interest it would have earned—that is the sum total of the loss to the economy. Data suggests that only 10 per cent of the annual black income generation goes abroad as flight of capital. Further, the amount mentioned does not mean that $2 trillion is lying outside the country ready to be brought back into Indian coffers. As I have mentioned, this sum is the amount that has gone out over seven decades and includes the interest that it would have earned if it was invested in safe securities. Moreover, a substantial part of this amount would have been brought back to the country via 'round tripping' (of which more later), consumed, invested and so on. So only a small part would be available in banks abroad which could be brought back. All this needs further analysis.

The Size Of The Black Economy

As we have seen at the outset, the size of the black economy in India is enormous. It is so extensive because it is generated in every sector and activity in the economy. All the elite sections of society are involved in it. It is in both the public and the private sectors. As the scams of the last three decades reveal, those involved include the families of top politicians (including prime ministers and chief ministers), major industrialists, generals, judges, bureaucrats, lawyers, academics, doctors and so on.

An indication of the fact that the black economy is growing is the rapid unearthing of more and bigger scams. While the biggest scam prior to 1990 was the Bofors Scam at ₹64 crore, in the 1990s there were many scams that were above ₹1,000 crore. The largest was the Harshad Mehta-led Stock Market Scam of 1991-1992, estimated by the Janakiraman Committee Report at ₹3,128 crore. In the first decade of this century, there was a flood of revelations of major scams—almost one a week—not counting the smaller cases of corruption involving a few crore rupees or less. Now the scams run into tens of thousands of crores of rupees and at times touch lakhs of crores of rupees. In the allotment of natural resources, like mines and spectrum, huge scams have been unearthed. Entire sections of the elite of our society seem to be involved.

Besides scams, the other activity that generates media headlines is tax evasion. What is revealing is that the tax evaders who are caught are not even a fraction of those who avoid paying taxes. It is estimated that taxes not collected at current rates of taxes would amount to about ₹37 lakh crore in 2016-2017. Were these taxes added to the government's coffers the budget, instead of showing a fiscal deficit, could have shown a surplus of about ₹30 lakh crore. There would then be no shortage of funds for employment generation, education, health and the creation of critical infrastructure like roads and power.

Consequences Of The Black Economy

In our country, people in their day-to-day dealings with the government or private organizations that provide services like electricity, phone and gas connections, healthcare and so on, face constant harassment. For the general public, illegality and corruption is a constant feature of their lives and they feel helpless in rectifying the situation. This is because every government that has been elected to power has been corrupt, and has fostered corruption for its own benefit.

A change in the ruling party only means that another corrupt setup comes to power. As a result, large sections of society mostly vote for their own corrupt political groups, so they have someone in power who can help them—Dalits vote for their own, the backward castes try to get their brethren into positions of power, Muslims favour their own community, and upper-caste Hindus have their own calculations. That is why today corruption as an election issue has been marginalized. Politicians of every hue might make a big show of being concerned about corruption but in reality they have no intention of cutting off sources of their own path to power. And when they are out of power all they need to do is wait patiently for their turn to come around again. This politics of corruption, where there is no determined effort to root out the malaise, means it flourishes at every level of society. When the law-providers are themselves to blame, it is small wonder that no other section of society feels the need to reform itself. We will look at this aspect of the black economy and its consequences a little later in the book.

Accuracy Of Data And Difficulties In Analysis

Many argue that there is little data on the black economy or that what is available is unreliable, so it is difficult to analyse the black economy, let alone its impact on the overall economy. The reality is that estimates about the black economy are based on macroeconomic parameters. But even data on the white economy is estimated since no one goes to each person to ask for the facts. It is true that the data on the black economy has larger errors than that of the white economy, but it must be kept in mind that estimates of the latter too are not accurate.

The biggest problem is that the black economy vitiates the data of the white economy. For instance, since people evade taxes by under-reporting their incomes, they show higher costs (like employment) and lower revenue. Thus, the data on employment and output is vitiated to the extent of the fudging of data for the generation of black incomes. So if we do not have the data on the impact of the black economy on income and employment, the white economy data on these variables becomes vitiated.

Theoretically, the black economy needs to be taken into account even if the data is weak. Its implications for all the major macro and microeconomic variables need to be understood if policies are to work. For instance, if monetary policies or fiscal policies are to succeed, the impact of the black economy has to be factored in. Similarly, if health and education policies are to deliver the expected outcomes then the impact of the black economy on these sectors needs to be taken into account. Theory will tell what kind of impact there will be while accurate data will tell the extent of the impact.

◆

Following this brief preamble, I'd like to examine various aspects of the black economy according to the scheme laid out earlier in the introduction. As this book is meant for the general reader, I have tried, wherever possible, to eschew jargon or academic terminology. Some financial and economic terms used in the text have been explained at the end of the book. I have also cut back on data, footnotes and other such aspects that would be more suited to a textbook or academic volume, retaining only the bare minimum to make my arguments.

I

WHAT IS THE BLACK ECONOMY?

To be able to analyse the black economy, it is important to comprehend the phenomenon one is talking about. Different people have different ideas about what they are referring to when they talk about the black economy. Thus, often there is cross talk and agreement becomes difficult. A proper understanding is needed to both measure the size of the black economy and to talk of its impact on society. Without this understanding one cannot understand the causes or talk of the remedies.

International studies show that the black economy is referred to by more than thirty different names all over the world—black money, parallel economy, informal economy, unaccounted economy, illegal economy, subterranean economy, and so on. However, none of these are appropriate terms to describe the black economy in India.

I.1.1 Black Money

Black money refers to cash saved from one's black income. Of the income one earns, a part is consumed and the rest is saved. The savings are invested to add to one's wealth. This wealth consists of all kinds of assets like shares, real estate, inventory in business and capital invested in business; only a small part is held as cash. Cash is usually used as working capital to pay wages to workers or to purchase things needed to carry on business. Only those who are not businessmen keep cash under their mattresses and even they often lend it to others for business and earn a return.

The common notion that the black economy means cash is not an accurate description. Essentially, the black economy consists of activities through which black incomes are earned. So, the black economy is about earning incomes (which is a flow) and not the holding of cash (a stock). Think of an overhead tank at home. This tank might hold a lot of water but the flow from it may be meagre. Alternatively, it is also possible that it has a small amount of water but the flow is large. So, if one is trying to determine how large a country's black economy is, one must understand that stocks do not necessarily tell us about the flow. Hence, it is incorrect to use the term black money to refer to the black economy.

I.1.2 Parallel Economy

Parallel economy is another commonly used term. This term implies two lines that meet at infinity or, in other words, never meet. It is used because people think that the black and the white economy are separate from each other. Nothing could be further from the truth, since in India the black and the white economy are intertwined. From the same economic activity one generates a black income and a white income. When one buys real estate, one has to pay the black component (say, 40 per cent) first and then the white component. So the seller earns a black and a white income simultaneously. Similarly, if cement producers under-invoice production by a certain percentage then they generate a black income from the undeclared production and a white income from the declared production. The two incomes are simultaneously generated.

Not only are the black and the white incomes generated through the same activity but one can also convert one's black income into white and vice versa. One can obtain from a broker a book entry in, say, the share market. By registering a profit one can convert one's black to white. Similarly, by taking a loss, one can convert white into black. So, someone's black becomes white and another's white becomes black.

I.1.3 Informal Economy

Westerners think of the black economy as an 'informal' economy. People in those parts of the world do a second or a third job and the income that they get from this activity is not reported for tax purposes; this is called the black economy. This activity is distinct from the formal job that one does to earn one's main income and that is why it is also referred to as the parallel economy. Most of one's formal or main activity is taxable. While the little extra income from one's informal activity is also taxable, as it is not declared, tax is evaded. In advanced economies, taxation begins at a low multiple of the per capita income, often even at one quarter of it. Thus, almost everyone is in the tax net, including those who are below the poverty line; informal sector incomes also become taxable.

In India, taxation begins at a high multiple of per capita income, say two or three times. Because of deductions and concessions available, people only begin to pay taxes at four to five times the per capita income. So, most people are out of the tax net. That is why out of a population of almost 130 crore, only about 5.2 crore people are in the tax net. Even then the number of people who actually pay significant tax is only about 1.5 crore (1.2 per cent of the population) as the rest file either a low return or a nil return. Thus, the tax base is very narrow.

Further, 94 per cent of the workforce is in the unorganized or informal sector (as per the Economic Survey) and earns very low incomes. A bulk of them are in agriculture and earn an income way below the taxable limit. Thus, whether they declare their income or not, they do not have to pay tax, and, therefore, cannot be said to be earning a black income.

In India, black income is earned in a number of ways. In the informal sector people such as the owner of a dhaba on a busy highway, say, at Murthal, Haryana, or a paan shop owner in a posh hotel and others engaged in similar activity would have taxable incomes but they may not be in the tax net, hence they can be said to be generating a black income. Thus, a part of the unorganized sector does generate black income but the vast majority of the people in this sector cannot be said to be generating a black income.

Many in the formal sector generate large amounts of black income. Corporates, self-employed professionals, transporters, financiers, builders, brokers, contractors and the like generate black income. Thus, to call the black economy an 'informal economy' is not appropriate in the Indian context. Black incomes are generated in both the formal and the informal sectors of the economy.

I.1.4 Illegal Economy

A country's economy comprises various activities that its citizens engage in. One can be an agriculturist or a self-employed professional or a businessperson or a manufacturer. An activity which is allowed by law is called legal while that which is not allowed by law is an illegal activity. For instance, narcotic drug dealing, sex work, gambling, smuggling, theft, etc. are all illegal activities. Illegal activities are not counted in the national income because they are supposed to have a negative impact on society.

In the national income one counts 'goods and services'. These are linked to the welfare of society and that is why they are characterized as 'good'—that is, they signify a social good. In contrast, illegal activities are taken as generating social 'bads' which adversely affect the welfare of individuals. Illegal activity generates an income that cannot be declared for tax purposes and, therefore, constitutes a black income. But, as we have seen, there are also a large number of people engaged in perfectly legal activity who generate black income by not declaring a part of their income; when they do this they commit an illegality. Examples of this would include a restaurant not declaring a part of its sales or teachers not declaring their tuition income. Therefore, in a country like India, black income comprises wholly illegal activity generating black income, as well as legal activities generating black income by committing an illegality which results in tax evasion.

I.1.5 Unaccounted Economy

The black economy is often thought of as being the unaccounted part of the economy. But what is the accounted part of the economy? The economy is made up of the Primary, Secondary and Tertiary sectors. These are further broken down into nine major sectors. The contribution from each of these sectors is added up to get the total national income. All this is to be found in the National Accounts Statistics (NAS). National income (loosely referred to as the GDP or gross domestic product) is estimated using different methods to account for the contribution of various sectors of the economy. It is usually assumed that the white economy is accounted for while the black economy is unaccounted. A little reflection shows that this is not true.

For instance, the contribution of agriculture is measured by the crop cutting experiment. This involves the measurement of the production from sample fields all over the country and then multiplying that by the total acreage under that crop. So, estimation does not depend on anyone reporting their output from their field. Thus, whether the agriculturists report their income or not, it is captured.

Similarly, in the construction sector, the contribution is measured by the product flow method. This method involves the use of the knowledge of six major inputs into construction, like steel, cement and so on. It is calculated how much of these inputs are needed to produce the buildings. This knowledge is then applied to work out the total use of these inputs to estimate the total production in the construction sector. So, even the black income generated in construction gets counted. However, this sector has a large unorganized or informal sector, for which the data is not easily available. So, the incomes generated there are estimated with reference to the activity in the organized sector; thus, it is an indirect method. However, it must be said that very often the incomes generated in the informal sector are missed out since the indirect method used is not satisfactory.

The entire unorganized sector is characterized by such deficiencies in method and inadequacy of data. Since, as explained earlier, the incomes of the unorganized sector are typically white incomes, one can argue that all the white incomes do not get counted. The problem is most severe in the case of services provided by the informal sectors.

Thus, the total national income is a mix of the white and black incomes while what is not counted is also a mix of the two. Which is why it is incorrect to simply say that black income is unaccounted income while white is accounted income.

I.1.6 Transfer and Factor Incomes

An economy produces goods and services. These are produced, distributed and financed to reach the consumer. But in any economy there is also the sale of property which leads to the transfer of assets from one person to the other. Thus, two kinds of incomes are generated in the economy. The first kind is linked to production and distribution and is called 'factor' income. The second kind is called 'transfer' income— this is generated through the sale and purchase of assets. No production is associated with these activities (except for a tiny amount of brokerage).

The production of any good or service requires the hiring of workers. These workers are paid wages.

When a product that has been made is sold a profit is generated. Thus, factor incomes generated through production are wages and profits. Rent, dividend and interest are counted as part of the profits and these may be broadly referred to as property (not to be confused with real estate) incomes. These incomes are earned on the ownership of some asset—rent is earned through ownership of land and buildings, dividend due to ownership of shares in companies, interest through ownership of financial instruments, and profits through the ownership of businesses. Wages also include the salaries paid to the managers, so they are called wages and salaries.

As we have seen, transfer incomes are in the nature of paper gains, independent of production. When a property is sold, it goes to the buyer and the seller gets the savings of the buyer. A pure transfer of assets is involved. This is the case with a real estate sale or the sale of a share in the secondary stock market. Similarly, in the case of a payment of a bribe, a transfer takes place from the bribe-giver to the bribe-receiver. The bribe-giver has to generate the black income and savings from it in some activity or the other and this is then transferred to the bribe-receiver. It could also be that the bribe-giver is using his white savings to give the bribe and in the process converting it into black.

Let us delve further into how transfer incomes are dealt with when it comes to counting a country's income. As asset prices rise, say, for real estate or in the case of shares, a capital gain is made. This is a paper gain which can reverse as asset prices can also fall. That is why these incomes are not counted in the national income; only factor incomes are counted. If this is not done, when the share market booms, as happened during the Harshad Mehta years in 1991-1992 or during the dot com boom in the year 2000, the national income will rise by a large per cent. The growth rate could be even 50 per cent. When these booms turn into busts, income growth would collapse and becomes negative. Such fluctuations due to paper gains are an additional reason why transfer incomes are not to be counted in the national income, but the main reason is that they are not related to production.

Finally, since transfer incomes are not counted in the white economy they should also not be counted in the black economy. After all, the black economy is calculated as a percentage of the white economy so the definition of the two should be comparable. This is why capital gains in real estate and stock markets and bribes have to be kept out of any calculation of the black income of a country.

However, it is a common misconception that real

estate is the biggest generator of black income. Even the Government of India made this elementary error. Be that as it may, not counting transfer incomes when calculating the national income or the size of the black economy does not mean that transfer incomes do not have an economic impact. They lead to a redistribution of incomes. When paper gains are made, people feel wealthier which results in higher consumption. So it needs to be understood that while transfer incomes are not counted as part of the national income/white economy and do not affect the income total, they do have other effects on the economy.

We will take a closer look at the aspect of factor incomes in the appendix where I examine how black incomes are to be identified.

I.1.7 Multiple Counting of Incomes to be Avoided

When sugar is produced and consignments of it go out of the factory gate, excise duty is supposed to be paid. When this consignment passes through a city, octroi (or entry tax) is supposed to be paid. When it is sold, a sales tax is supposed to be paid. After the sale takes place, a profit is generated on which a corporation tax is supposed to be paid. Of the profit that remains, which is called net profit, a dividend is supposed to be distributed to the shareholders who are liable to pay an income tax on the income they receive. (This income tax is now paid by the company, but nonetheless a tax is supposed to be paid.)

Thus, if the production of sugar is understated and black profits are generated, five taxes are evaded. If we count the incomes associated with all the taxes that are being evaded then we will count the black income generation five times. This is incorrect and can be called the 'multiple counting' of black incomes. (But this is what the tax man is interested in. He wants to know how much tax is not being paid. However, analytically, we cannot adopt that stance.)

When production takes place in the white economy, even though five taxes are paid, the income is counted only once since that is the factor income generated through production. Thus, when calculating the size of the black economy one should count only the factor income that is evaded and not the number of incomes on which taxes are evaded. From each of the factor incomes evaded we can calculate how much tax is evaded by adding all the taxes that are evaded. But, as the name black income suggests, we are interested in the income evaded. (The amount of tax evaded is another matter, though relevant for fiscal policy and so on.)

I.1.8 Mechanism of Black Income Generation

When we buy something from a shopkeeper we pay them a price. This is their revenue and not their income because they have to incur costs to stock, finance and sell the product. The income of any businessperson is then the revenue minus the cost incurred. So,

$$Profit\ (P) = Rev\ (R) - Cost\ (C)$$

This profit is split into two parts. One that is declared in the balance sheet of the enterprise and the other that is not declared and is called the off-balance sheet profit. Many businesses maintain two books of accounts, one for income tax purposes and another for themselves. So,

$$White\ Profit\ (P_w) = Balance\ Sheet\ Profit = Declared\ R - Declared\ C$$

Off-balance sheet profit is the black income earned by mis-invoicing revenues and costs. Usually, revenues are under-reported while the costs are overstated. If a businessperson sells 10 tons of cement at ₹100 per ton, they may report only 9 tons sold and at a price of ₹90. The difference between the actual revenue of ₹1,000 and the one that is reported, ₹810, is siphoned off as undeclared profit.

Similarly, costs of all kinds can be overstated. So,

wages can be shown to be higher than those actually paid or the number of workers the company employs inflated. This was the case in muster roll fudging in the Employment Guarantee Scheme and in the scheme under the Mahatma Gandhi National Rural Employment Guarantee Act (MGNREGA). This sort of chicanery was also found in the case of the Satyam Scam which broke in 2009—the IT company reportedly had 13,000 fictitious employees on its rolls. The wage bill is shown to be higher and this is siphoned off as a personal profit of the contractor or the management. Other ways of generating unaccounted income include reporting higher raw material costs and overheads than is actually the case. The personal travel expenses of owners and the salaries of household staff they employ and so on are reported as company expenses. This is why it is said that while companies go sick the managements prosper.

Putting all this together, we have:

$$Black\ Profit\ (P_b) = Off\text{-}Balance\ Sheet\ Profit = Undeclared\ R + Overstated\ C$$

The significance of this formulation is that black incomes are factor incomes, property incomes (as defined earlier) and not wage incomes. This is because wages are a cost to businesses so they over-report them. Consequently, the black economy leads to the under-reporting of profits while wages are overstated. To sum up:

a. The distribution of incomes between profits and wages in the economy is more skewed than what is estimated from the white economy data.
b. Employment is overstated in the official data.
c. Costs are overstated while the output is under-reported so that the input–output ratio (how much input cost is incurred to produce one unit of output) is incorrect. It is higher in the white economy than the actual.
d. A small amount of output evasion leads to a large amount of black-income generation since the production of undeclared output is costless.
e. Capital is overstated while the output is understated so that the incremental capital output ratio of the white economy is overstated.
f. Taxes paid are lower than they could be, thereby reducing the tax/GDP ratio below what it could be potentially.
g. As should be clear from the foregoing, the basic difference between black income generation in developing and advanced countries has to do with the fact that in the latter, factor income, wages, is the main generator of black income whereas in the

former it accrues from property (which, as we have seen, is not the same thing as real estate) income. These results have major consequences for the entire economy and not just the black economy.

I.2 DEFINITION

The above formulation makes clear that black incomes in India are factor incomes, property incomes. As discussed, if one tax is evaded then all the way to the end the other taxes are also evaded. So, if excise duty is evaded on some output then the sales tax, income tax and other taxes will also be evaded. As argued earlier, there should not be multiple counting of taxes evaded. Only the income associated with the final tax evaded, namely the direct tax, need be counted.

Thus, the definition we arrive at of the black economy is: *The black economy consists of all the activities in which black incomes are generated and black incomes are factor incomes, property incomes, not reported to direct tax authorities.*

I first defined the black economy in this way in 1999 and measured its size as per this definition. Others measured something else and called it the black economy. Thus, all the other available measures are not consistent in definition so that a comparison of different estimates is like comparing apples and oranges. There is, therefore, a lot of inconsistency and confusion about the way in which the black economy should be measured. I look at this in some detail in the appendix. Before we move on, let us explicate my definition of the black economy a little further.

The exception to the above definition is wage incomes in the illegal sector which are also black incomes since the entire income in these sectors is black income. This would be the case even though most of the wages paid in the illegal sector would be below the taxable limit.

Agriculture bears no income tax, so these incomes are not required to be reported to tax authorities and, therefore, there is no question of generating black income in this sector. However, income from other sectors may be diverted and shown as agricultural income to escape taxation. These incomes should be counted where they are generated rather than as agricultural black income. If not, there would be double counting and this would result in fouling up the calculation.

Most of the black incomes are generated in the services sector, as mentioned earlier, by manipulating accounts to show lower property incomes. It turns out that the services sector generates the largest amount of black incomes. As it is, there is a large gap between per person incomes in agriculture and services, and the black economy aggravates this further. In the white economy the contribution of agriculture now is about 14 per cent and that of the services sector is close to 60 per cent. If the black economy is added to the white economy then the contribution of agriculture comes down to 8 per cent of GDP while that of the services sector rises to close to 80 per cent (like in the advanced economies).

I.3 MEASURING THE BLACK ECONOMY

To complete the definition of the black economy we should also have a sense of the various ways in which it is measured. However, as this is a rather technical discussion, I have placed it at the end of the book as the appendix. For a broad understanding of what is meant by measuring the overall economy and the black economy there are two aspects to be considered. The first is whether data is available to be measured and the second is the way in which the data is interpreted. It is often argued that as there is no reliable data it is impossible to analyse the black economy and its impact on the overall economy. However, even if there is little or no data available on the black economy that does not mean we should not be talking about it, or attempting to measure and define it. The debate between economists

Paul Baran and Nicholas Kaldor is instructive in this respect. While reviewing Baran's book, *The Political Economy of Growth*, Kaldor had critiqued the notion of 'potential economic surplus' by arguing that we know what the actual surplus is but we cannot measure the potential economic surplus so it is futile to talk about it. Baran's riposte was that we know a bottle of brandy consists of alcohol and water; however, as we cannot separate the two, is it correct to say that brandy is only water or only alcohol? Both these definitions are incorrect and so we have to say that brandy contains both water and alcohol even if (for the purpose of argument) we cannot tell how much of each there is in the bottle. In similar fashion, the black economy needs to be taken into account when we talk of the overall economy even if the data is weak.

The problem of data aside, what is the methodology that is used to determine the quantum of the black economy? I go into greater detail about this in the appendix but, broadly speaking, we know that the black economy in aggregate is stated to be a percentage of the white economy (GDP). Separate components of the black economy such as income earned in education, law and so on are given in absolute numbers but we know this is difficult to determine accurately as people do not come forward to report their black income. We have already looked at the various ways in which white income is estimated in the various sectors in National Account Statistics. A roughly similar approach is followed to estimate the size of black income.

The methods used are called trace methods since one looks for traces of the black economy in the visible white economy rather like Sherlock Holmes looking for tell-tale clues while investigating a murder. The four main trace methods are: 1) survey approach; 2) input-output method; 3) monetarist approach; and 4) fiscal approach. These are discussed in greater detail in the appendix.

Of all these approaches the fiscal approach is the correct approach to use to determine the size of the black economy as this approach is based on the various institutional factors of the economy and takes into account the differences across various sectors. It separates the illegal from the legal sectors. It treats agriculture differently from non-agricultural sectors. It takes into account the presence of the large informal sector where incomes are mostly below the taxable limit. It also differentiates between wage income and property income. Using the fiscal approach, the size of the black economy was estimated to be 4-5 per cent of GDP in 1955, 7 per cent in 1970, 18 per cent in 1980-1981 and 40 per cent in 1995-1996. This last estimate includes 8 per cent contributed by illegal activities like drugs, extortion and smuggling. A further 32 per cent is generated from legal activities like, manufacturing, finance, trade and construction. Extrapolating from here, I arrived at my estimate of the figure of the black economy in 2012-2013 as 62 per cent of GDP. Assuming that it has remained the same for 2016-2017, it works out to ₹93 lakh crore.

II

THE BLACK ECONOMY
IN INDIA TODAY

II.1 ECONOMIC ASPECTS

Most of the key economic problems India faces can be linked to the existence of a large black economy. This should not occasion surprise, for no economy can thrive where billions of dollars are spirited out, black transactions abound in the stock and real-estate markets, and where even matters like getting admission for schoolchildren requires bribes. What is being revealed by official agencies or in the media with relentless regularity is only the tip of the iceberg.

Due to the black economy, government policy fails and society is unable to achieve its goals, especially in critical areas like literacy and health. Consequently, a vast majority of Indians live in miserable conditions. For all the big talk of party spokespersons and the pseudo-nationalism displayed by ruling party cheerleaders, the unfortunate truth is that today the quality of life of an extremely large number of Indians is poorer than that found in most parts of the world. Worse, most of the schemes floated by governments have done little or nothing to improve the situation. This is because of the negative impact of the black economy.

As finance minister in the UPA government P. Chidambaram said in his budget speech in 2005: 'outlays [expenditures] do not necessarily mean outcomes'. In 1987, Prime Minister Rajiv Gandhi said that out of every rupee sent to the field, only 15 paise reached the ultimate recipient it was intended for. (It must be clarified though, that he did not mean that all of it was lost due to corruption, bureaucratic inefficiencies also contributed to this dissipation.)

The failure of government spending is not the only thing the black economy impacts. It is also the reason why government policy is not implemented in a way that benefits citizens. Whether it is environmental regulation or industrial location or urban zoning or traffic lights, all laws are routinely violated. No wonder that at a low level of per capita income, India has some of the worst air and water pollution in the world. Due to insanitary conditions and water pollution, most people suffer from poor health resulting in low labour productivity. Literacy is low because money sent for constructing schools is often siphoned off and teachers are either not appointed or absent themselves. According to a Pratham report, 50 per cent of schoolchildren in the fifth grade are unable to read grade two books, and as a result are condemned to work at low levels of productivity for the rest of their lives and are likely to remain poor.

The effects of the black economy are not just felt by economically deprived sections of our society, but impact the work ethic of elite sections of society too. Given the hurdles that have to be overcome at every step, Indians do not achieve (with few exceptions) world standards in anything, whether in sports or in technology. As has been shown, this is not because there is a lack of resources, but because these resources are either siphoned off or poorly deployed. As the situation worsens, individual citizens are alienated from society, making any sustained or collective action to turn things around difficult.

II.1.1 Characterization of the Black Economy and Increasing Inefficiency

About two decades ago, I wrote that many aspects of the black economy are like the phenomenon of 'digging holes and filling them'. Allow me to explain: if during the day, a person is set to work to dig a hole and at night another person is employed to fill it up, the next morning there is zero output—but two people have earned incomes for the work they have done. In other words, there is activity without productivity. Assets are not created commensurate with the activity or the expenditures. As we noted earlier, when sub-standard material is used for the construction of roads, they get damaged and potholed with the first spell of rain and have to be repaired. Consequently, a large part of the road budget is spent on repair work rather than building new roads for, say, rural connectivity.

In schools, ill-paid teachers teach poorly so students neither learn nor enjoy classes. They get put off from learning and divert their attention to other things. When they go home they are forced to take tuition so as to do well in examinations. Many teachers have a vested interest in not teaching well so that they can take tuitions to make extra money. The result is that students begin to find school difficult and learn things by rote and don't understand them. The tutors also focus on getting their students to pass exams rather than building an understanding. They stop questioning and lose their curiosity about life. Their time is wasted, first in class and then at tuition. Time that could have been used for other activities and for learning is frittered away. All this results in a massive waste of resources for the nation since the outcome with regard to learning is poor. Further, it leads to students of indifferent quality in higher education and industry complaints of lack of employability of a large number of graduates. Consequently, in spite of the large numbers of students in higher education, India produces few who are internationally competitive.

Such examples of waste are all around us. Take the judiciary, for example, where cases go on for years even though they are supposed to be resolved in months. The police often do not register cases and harass the public. Cases are poorly investigated and in the end they are thrown out by the courts so that justice is not done in spite of the efforts of many people. In the end, the individual has to pay bribes and grease the wheels of the system to get justice. The black economy therefore has both a direct and indirect effect here.

The net result is that there is 'social waste' and the impact of investment in the economy is lowered. So, effectively, it is like having less investment than shown on paper.

◆

The other characterization of the black economy I have given is that it makes 'the usual the unusual and the unusual the usual'—it implies that which should occur does not and that which should not, often does. For instance, citizens who should get 220 volts in their electricity supply either get say, 170 volts or an excess, say, 270 volts and as a result their expensive electronic equipment burns out. To prevent this, one needs additional circuits in the equipment or voltage stabilizers which means that capital costs rise. In addition, the cost of servicing equipment rises as the breakdown rate increases. The fluctuating voltage and variable cycles of supply of electricity also lead to poor quality production since machines can malfunction. In the case of goods manufactured through continuous flow production—for example, chemicals—such malfunctions can lead to clogged lines and wastage.

One should be able to get clean drinking water in the taps but it is more often than not polluted because the pipelines may be of poor quality or not properly laid out, causing sewage to seep in. Thus, one has to incur additional expenditure in boiling water or using purifiers of various descriptions or buying bottled water at hundreds of times the cost of the content. Even then, a little carelessness could lead to water-borne diseases and infections, meaning more and unnecessary expenditure on health and safety.

Then there are services which citizens should ordinarily get from the bureaucracy—such as correct tax assessment, getting a passport or a driving licence, admission to schools and professional courses, railway reservations—but due to harassment, they have to approach touts and pay extra. As one cannot fight corruption continuously, eventually one gives in and pays that extra cost to influence the outcome. Further, since one has to pay everywhere, there is pressure to join in and make money where one's position enables one to do so. Every time this happens, illegality and the black economy get a boost.

II.1.2 Macroeconomic Aspects

As we have seen, black incomes comprise factor incomes, property incomes that are not reported to direct tax authorities. What escapes the indirect tax net is also not reported to the direct tax authorities. Hence production is only partially captured in the white economy data. Further, as we have seen, illegal activities are not reportable, hence they are completely out of the tax net and entirely black. It has been shown that wages are inflated to show higher costs and generate black incomes. Revenues are shown to be less through under-invoicing and wages (costs) are over-invoiced (shown to be higher). Hence, profits are shown to be lower while wages are shown to be higher. Consequently, the income distribution is more skewed than depicted by the white economy data.

Further, as the black economy grows relative to the white economy, the share of profits rises. Since profits tend to be much larger than the wages, the share of high incomes rises and since more is saved out of high incomes, the share of savings in the economy rises. This is important since it has an impact on incomes in the economy via the investment multiplier. The investment multiplier tells us how many times of the investment is the national income. This multiplier is the inverse of the savings rate in the economy, so it falls as the share of black economy rises. Consequently, as the black economy grows, for a given level of investment in the economy, the level of income is lower.

It has also been shown that the rate of investment in the economy falls due to the black economy. This is a result of a) capital going abroad via flight of capital. So instead of capital being invested in India it is invested abroad and leads to shortage of capital in the country; b) due to the 'digging holes and filling holes' phenomenon, the value of investment is effectively less than it should be, as explained earlier; c) there is over-invoicing of capital so that what is recorded is more than actual and so on. To explain, a businessman investing in an industry claims to have invested, say, ₹100 crore whereas they may have only invested ₹80 crore. The extra amount of ₹20 crore is siphoned off. This is called over-invoicing of capital and results in the generation of black income. The decline in the overall level of investment results in a lower level of output in the economy.

The actual input-output ratio of the economy is lower than that suggested by the white economy. This results in problems of planning and failure in execution. In simple terms, suppose the government is planning for 100 while the economy is actually 162 (because of the black economy), so the state is planning for the wrong amount of requirement of steel, energy, transportation and so on.

The incremental capital-output ratio rises because of the inefficient use of capital due to the black economy. The rate of growth that is achieved is, therefore, lower than the potential rate of growth. (The potential rate of growth is the rate of growth which could be achieved if the black economy is eliminated so that the productivity of investment becomes higher and the level of investment rises.) The graph below shows just how much better off the country would be without the black economy.

Actual and Hypothetical Index of GDP

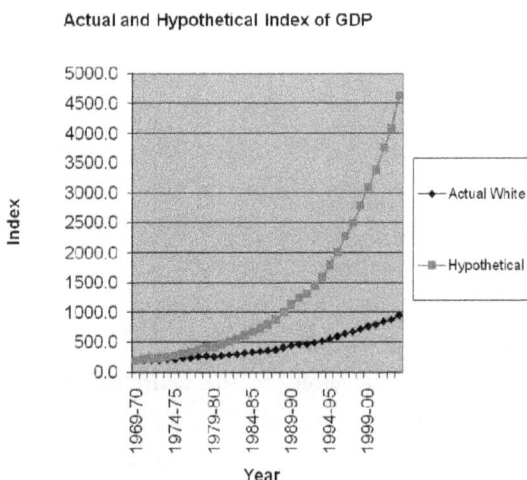

This explains the seeming paradox that while the black economy leads to a higher level of output, employment and growth rate, it actually lowers the level of employment and output and rate of growth compared to the potential of the economy. What it means is that the actual rate of growth is higher than that shown by the white economy but lower than the potential rate of growth. The reason is that productivity of investment is lowered by the black economy due to wasteful investment and misuse of capital as argued above. This can be captured by the following formulation:

$$r_p > r_b > r_a > r_w$$

where r_p stands for the potential, r_b for the black, r_a for the actual and r_w for the white economy rates of growth respectively.

Thus, although the black economy generates output and employment, far more is lost than gained.

Monetary policy is adversely affected since the money available in the economy has to circulate the black economy (in addition to the white economy). Money has to go around faster than if there was only the white economy. Additional liquidity in the economy is required but that is not captured by the official data since it is not factored into the equations used by the Reserve Bank of India (RBI). Consequently, the velocity of circulation—i.e. how many times money has to change hands in a year—calculated with white economy data turns out to be incorrect. The consequence is that it becomes difficult to control inflation. For example, if there is a shortage of, say, onions, it is exacerbated by the inflow of black liquidity which aggravates the shortage. Thus, if the shortage was actually 10 per cent, it could rise to 25 per cent because suppliers simply hold their stocks of onions in anticipation of the increase in prices. If at 10 per cent shortage the price was to rise by 25 per cent, with a 25 per cent shortage the price rise could be as high as 400 per cent. Even if 10 per cent of the onion stocks rots due to poor storage, the traders stand to make a killing. Under these circumstances, even if the RBI tightens money supply it does not help. The issue does not remain a purely monetary policy matter but becomes one of political management. So the principal task of the RBI, namely controlling inflation, slips out of its hands.

◆

The adverse effect of the black economy can also be seen in the Balance of Payments (BOP) scenario. BOP refers to a nation's situation regarding its trade of goods and services and capital flows in relation to all other nations. It is adversely affected due to various factors linked to the black economy. For instance, due to under-invoicing of exports the nation's exports are shown to be less and its trade deficit becomes larger. It can be shown that the white economy data does not capture activities like under- and over-invoicing of trade in goods and services. There are also illegal flows due to illicit activities like drugs and gunrunning. Flows through the parallel banking channel, called hawala, are left out. Thus, even though

India does not have capital account convertibility—which means that people cannot automatically buy foreign exchange with the rupees they have—due to the black economy, one can convert rupees to foreign exchange. This results in policy failure not only on the trade front but more broadly on the macroeconomic front. These illegal transactions are difficult to track and estimate due to the phenomena of 'layering' and 'round tripping'. This can be written as the following equation:

$$BOP_{actual} = BOP_{legal} + BOP_{illegal}$$

Effectively, the flight of capital associated with the black economy is the main cause of the BOP problems that have plagued the Indian economy since Independence.

As we have seen, all of this has serious consequences for fiscal policy due to the shortfall of revenue collection and inflation of expenditures. Thus, the deficits in the budgets are higher than they need be. The black economy results in loss of revenue of about 25 per cent of GDP at current rates of taxes. In comparison, the fiscal deficit is currently around 4 per cent of GDP for the centre. Had the black economy not existed, the revenue deficit which underlies the fiscal deficit and rising debt in the budget would have been wiped out so that the fiscal health of the government would have been better. If the black economy had been white, there would have been a surplus in the budget and there would have been much greater investments in infrastructure and poverty removal. Also, with less corruption, expenditures would have been more effective.

There is a shortage of resources for plans, capital expenditure and essentials like education and health. Indirect taxes are high and borrowings larger than they need be. The latter results in higher interest outgo and over time it has increased so much that it has become the largest component of the revenue budget. So we borrow money with one hand and return it with the other.

Due to inflation of costs, prevailing black margins and higher indirect taxes, the rate of inflation is higher than it need be. The quality of production is poor and this leads to the waste of resources and lower competitiveness in the export markets.

In brief, India's macroeconomy cannot be correctly understood without taking the black economy into account. For most empirical analyses the black economy that should be incorporated is not, so there is a gap in the analysis. For proper analysis the black economy is either a missing or a mis-specified variable.

II.1.3 Impact on Inequality and Poverty

In a study I made over two decades ago, I estimated

that the black economy was concentrated in the hands of, at most, 3 per cent of the population in 1995. Yes, there is petty corruption throughout society but this is insignificant compared to the black incomes earned by those in the upper echelons. It was assumed then that the bottom 40 per cent in the income ladder were around the poverty line. In 1995, if the ratio of incomes between the top 3 per cent and the bottom 40 per cent in the income ladder was 12:1 in the white economy, it became 57:1 if the black economy were included. The percentage of those earning substantial black incomes would only have increased since 1995. But if it is assumed that the percentage has remained the same (at about 3 per cent) and the fraction of those at the poverty line is also similar, the disparities would be much larger now given that the black economy has grown significantly and the disparities between the rich and the poor too have grown significantly after 1995.

Thus, today, in a vast and poor population of 1.27 billion, there are 39 million who are well off—the size of a European nation—who can afford all the luxuries, because many of them have large black incomes *in addition* to their high white incomes. This explains the existence of vast poverty in the midst of glitzy markets and the ostentatious consumerism of the wealthy. Another manifestation of such skewed income levels is (as discussed earlier) that the savings propensity of the overall economy is higher than recorded in the white economy. This is a consequence of the fact that the rich, with their high incomes, tend to save more than the poor who, of necessity, have to consume their entire income.

Absolute poverty is also impacted by the growth of the black economy. The increase in social waste has meant that the increase in GDP does not translate into a higher level of welfare of the people.

I have touched upon the indirect cost of the black economy, but let us go a little deeper into the issue. For example, the increased levels of pollution of water and air, due to the violation of environmental rules and regulations, has led to increased incidences of disease. This has especially impacted the poor, whose living conditions are deteriorating not only in the cities but also in the villages due to the excessive use of pesticides and chemical fertilizers, leading to the pollution of water bodies. The cost of treatment has risen sharply because of the liberalization of prices post 1991 and the decline in the public health system.

A study from Kerala, between 1987 and 1996, showed that there has been a 'mediflation' with increases not only medicine costs but also doctor's fees, laboratory charges, etc. The most disturbing aspect noted is the rapidly increasing financial burden on the poor. It is noted that for the well-off sections the rise was 326 per cent but for the poorest group it was 768 per cent and for the next higher category 1,002 per cent. The percentage of income spent rose for the rich from 2.18 to 2.44 but for the poor it went up from 7.18 to 39.63. In other words, even as things ostensibly change for the better, they are actually getting worse.

Education is being increasingly privatized, thereby raising the cost of education for all segments of society. While the very poor may not send their children to private schools, the slightly better off do. Thus, almost the entire gain in income has been wiped out for the poor by the increase in health costs and for the slightly better off the gain has been wiped out by the increased costs of education and health. Unfortunately, our wholesale price index (WPI) does not take health and education costs into account so our inflation index does not reflect these price increases. So while the official data may show an increase in real wages they may actually be falling when all prices are taken into account.

Finally, due to the demonstration effect of rampant consumerism among the wealthy who have benefitted from the black economy, the aspiration levels of the poor have risen and many of them also want to possess mobile phones, televisions and other components of 'achhe din'. In many parts of the country, these things have become the 'minimum necessary social consumption' and that changes the definition of the poverty line. After meeting these expenditures there is inadequate income left for food and other essentials. Add to this the rise of social evils such as alcoholism and drug abuse due to the pressure of keeping up with the modern pace of life and what it costs to sustain such habits among the poor, and it becomes clear that the deleterious effects of the black economy are far wider than it may seem at first glance.

Thus, while for the government poverty is declining because real wages have risen, the poverty line itself is changing due to the impact of the black economy and the demonstration effect associated with it. Put differently, it would be incorrect to say poverty is declining because what constitutes poverty is changing all the time. Not taking the black economy into account in policy-making makes the problem more intractable.

II.1.4 The Black Economy and Illicit Financial Flows

It has been estimated by a 2010 Global Financial Integrity (GFI) report that since Independence, $462 billion (₹31.5 lakh crore) has been lost to the nation due to illicit capital flows. This is equivalent to India's current foreign debt or the aid it has received since Independence.

However, in my view, this figure is an underestimate of the opportunity cost of illicit financial flows pertaining to India. As has been pointed out in a recent study, if one were to take into account illegal activities, services mispricing and transfer pricing, the actual figure may be around $2 trillion (₹136 lakh crore) for the period 1948 to 2012. These flows take place in many ways but very importantly through shell companies set up in tax havens (over ninety at current count) to launder the money siphoned out of the country. Hence they are difficult to detect or track.

Thus, a capital-short country has been losing capital on a large scale. It could be said that the drain of wealth during colonial rule has continued in a different form after Independence. Those indulging in the flight of capital include businessmen, corrupt politicians, bureaucrats, professionals and others. These are the people whose attachment to the country has weakened as their wealth abroad has increased and they often push the interests of foreign powers. They are also open to blackmail by foreign agencies who track the flow of illicit funds from and to India.

If the amount lost to the country due to illicit flows had been invested in the country, say, in rural areas that are woefully short of basic infrastructure like water, sanitation or electricity, the quality of life of the average Indian could have been far better than it is today. Alternatively, if this capital had been invested in industry, industrialization and technology, productivity could have been far greater than it is at present. Thus, the flight of capital associated with the black economy has resulted in India growing more slowly than it should have.

Of late, a phenomenon called 'round tripping', in which capital leaves the country and returns, has been noticed. In the late 1990s the software industry became the conduit for bringing back capital without paying taxes. Later, the Mauritius route was also added to facilitate this 'round tripping', of which more in Chapter V.

II.1.5. *Global Economic Flows*

Local criminal activities have been linked to transnational crimes through terrorism: the printing and circulation of counterfeit currencies; the operation of hawala; the production and distribution of narcotic drugs; arms-trafficking; and the smuggling of electronic items, gold and gems. In all these cases, our neighbouring countries, especially Pakistan, Afghanistan, Bangladesh and Myanmar—and at times their secret services—are involved. The profits from these activities help finance terrorism meant to destabilize the nation.

Myanmar was a closed nation till recently and there has been much ethnic conflict there. As a result, it was easy to move narcotic drugs through these territories into India's Northeast, where separatist movements were taking place. Similarly, Bangladesh has been another porous border through which human trafficking has been taking place and where terrorist movements had found sanctuary.

The conflict in Afghanistan, since the beginning of the 1970s, has resulted in that country becoming awash with weapons supplied by the West. Afghanistan is also a centre for the production of narcotic drugs. When the central power weakened and regional warlords emerged, the Taliban smuggled weapons and narcotics to finance and enrich themselves. A nexus then emerged between the Taliban and Muslim fundamentalists in Pakistan. This impacted the separatist movement in Kashmir and also became a major source of financing for Muslim fundamentalism in India. In the process, India became a part of transnational crime. This was facilitated by a corrupt bureaucracy and the police.

Smugglers developed links with organized crime abroad to carry on their activities systematically. These links required them to be in touch with hawala operators, who did not distinguish between clean (but illegal) money and dirty money. So they transferred the money of terrorists just as often as that of businessmen under-invoicing exports. In fact, gold smugglers often needed foreign currency to buy gold for smuggling into India, and they got it from drug rings that needed to send funds to finance their activities in India. Thus, many inter-linkages developed.

Smuggling was driven by the chance to make easy money. Smugglers flourished because of high custom duties for the import of luxury goods like liquor, tobacco products, gold and gems, and a ban on the import of other items. Airports and ports turned into dens of corruption with all kinds of illegal activities taking place. Very complex import rules were set up so that the misclassification of goods and services became possible. (The threat of harassment is an important driver for the willingness to bribe the officials.)

As a result of all this, hawala grew in size in India. It is not regulated by the central bank. It is used to transfer funds within the country and outside it. Since it deals purely in cash, large sums of money are moved through the premises from which hawala operations function. The police and the intelligence agencies know of these places, but they do not act because of high-level political protection available to the hawala operators. The top politicians in power also know of them, since they use this channel, but they do not act against these hawala operators out of self-interest.

◆

Everything we have discussed in this chapter has resulted in the alienation of the common man from the system. They assume nothing will work as expected and that they will need to pay extra to make things work. Even in a medical emergency it is often the case that one first calls up some friend or relative for advice as to where to go rather than going straight to the nearest hospital emergency room. Indeed, it is often a miracle that one survives a medical emergency since so many things can go wrong. In the event of a road accident few stop to take the victim to hospital lest they face harassment. In the hospital the doctors may wait for legal formalities to be completed before they begin treatment. They may do a slipshod job or the medicines may be spurious or sub-standard and may not have the desired effect, with the result that the outcome of the treatment is sub-optimal. All these things are so much a part of everyday life in India that people have lost faith in the system, in government, in collective action.

In many ways, this has led to a situation where individuals have come to believe in luck and God and prefer to look for hacks or jugaad solutions to their everyday problems rather than relying on the mechanisms that are supposed to regulate and improve the quality of their life in society. The net result is that democracy itself is weakened. These are some of the larger consequences that result from the existence of the black economy.

III

ORIGINS AND GROWTH

III.1 THE HISTORY OF THE BLACK ECONOMY

The black economy and illegality have existed in all societies at some point. In India, it became systematic during World War II, when shortages of essential items became critical. Rationing of food was introduced but black market activities also emerged. To escape detection, perpetrators bribed the bureaucracy and the police. Inflation led to increases in the price of property, meaning that those without property found it difficult to get housing. The government introduced rent control laws, which later on became a source of corruption in the courts.

The British set up a civil service to administer

(keep control of) India. The public servant became in effect the public master with enormous power over the people—this was used to extract bribes. However, as the bulk of the population was poor, self-employed, or worked in agriculture, civil servants had few dealings with the public, so the level of corruption and the black economy was negligible. Moreover, the civil service was accountable to the colonial masters. Because they were interested in efficient control of the country, they did not allow corruption to grow. They also paid the civil servants high salaries, as compared to the per capita incomes of locals, and gave them many privileges so they were less tempted to be corrupt.

There was a landlord class ruling over the peasantry that extracted rent from the farmers on behalf of the colonial masters. They were a part of the tiny colonial ruling elite and had substantial powers, which were misused to collect money from the people they ruled. In real terms, however, their depredations did not affect the economy too much as their numbers were not significant.

After Independence, an Indian political class came to power. They started the task of development in a very poor country. They depended on the civil service to govern the country and did not transform it into a public service that was accountable to the people. The political class that emerged from the national freedom movement was democratic in its aspirations, but its members came from the country's elite class and had feudal inclinations. They thought of themselves as rulers and not as true representatives of the people. Consequently, independent India started with high aspirations but a weak democracy because the power was transferred from the colonial masters to a relatively unaccountable political class and a civil service that was accountable mostly to the ruling elite. As the democratic aspirations of the national movement weakened, the political class became more corrupt. The Government of India report of 1956 argued for the need to keep the black economy in check so that more resources could be raised for development. It found businesses generating profits from black market activities in all sectors of the economy.

The Indian national movement understood that colonial rule was responsible for not only impoverishing the common man but was also the reason he was unable to better his lot. Therefore it was decided that society as a whole had to overcome these basic problems (poverty, education, health and so on) of the people and the state was given a large role in economic matters. The optimum utilization of resources required, among other things, central planning, which required the licensing of capacity in industries. This reinforced the role of the state in the economy.

Due to deindustrialization in India during colonial rule, Indian capitalists were too small to generate the capital necessary for the creation of the essential infrastructure for transportation and power, for example. They lacked the technology and capital to invest in basic goods like metals and petroleum, or in capital goods manufacturing. The corollary was that a large public sector was needed to support both the growth of the private sector and the planning process. This required the mobilization of savings in a country that was poor. Consequently, consumption had to be restrained through taxation and limiting the production and importation of luxury goods. Imports were limited so as to conserve the foreign exchange required to import capital goods for development. A strategy of import substitution was adopted to boost industry and high customs duties were introduced for this purpose.

In 1944, representatives of Indian big business drew up a plan of industrialization in post-independence India that contained the above-mentioned elements of policy. These plans were also incorporated in the industrial policy statements of 1948 and 1956. However, what the business class agreed to collectively, they undid through their private actions by fouling up policies through illegality. They cornered licenses by bribing authorities and creating monopolies for economic gain. Corruption was introduced into various development activities and projects in order to make extra profits. This would not have been feasible without the connivance of politicians and the bureaucracy. Luxury goods, or those goods that were either banned or faced high customs duties, were smuggled in.

As India developed, the size of the middle class increased and the shortages of basic goods (e.g. food, scooters, cement) or basic services (e.g. telephone and railway reservations) appeared. Queues formed for each of them, and soon thereafter black markets developed. Businesses took advantage of these black markets and corruption spread to the lower levels of society.

Big business in India realized that the manipulation of trade and economic policies required close proximity to political power. It started exercising direct control over the political process by financing political parties and individual candidates for legislatures. It also increasingly interfered in appointments at the senior levels of the bureaucracy in key ministries.

There was growth in illegal business practices in India during the oil crisis and a sharp increase in the petro goods prices in the 1970s. The sudden wealth generated by the oil-exporting countries, especially in West Asia, led to large-scale economic activities there, but as they lacked the necessary skilled labour (carpenters, plumbers, drivers, teachers, engineers, doctors), they imported it from South Asia on a large scale. These migrants started sending money back home to their families. This encouraged the spread of hawala internationally because the hawala operators provided cheap services and a premium on the money sent through them. Simultaneously, this service also allowed Indian businesses to send their capital abroad.

III.2. POST 1991 MARKETIZATION PHASE

In 1991, the government liberalized economic policies. This meant their marketization, namely allowing the greater play of the markets in the economy by reducing government intervention. Controls and regulations were greatly reduced throughout the economy.

Economic liberalization meant massive concessions to the private sector—whatever it had been demanding in the 1980s was granted. Direct taxes were reduced, licensing was eliminated, imports were liberalized, and so on. There was the elimination/reduction of controls such as restrictions under the Monopolies and Restrictive Trade Practices (MRTP) Act, Foreign Exchange Regulation Act (FERA), reservations and licensing. The role of the public sector and planning was minimized. With the establishment of the World Trade Organization (WTO) in 1995, there was a further opening up of the economy to foreign trade and capital. As the white economy grew, so did its black counterpart. But its nature changed. Anything could be imported, and the private sector was allowed to produce luxury goods. The shortages of telephones, automobiles, televisions, and other consumer goods disappeared, as did the black markets associated with them. But as restraints on business declined with the weakening of the state, businesses indulged in corruption on an even larger scale. For instance, they could take their money out more easily as exchange controls were relaxed. They could play around more easily in the financial markets to generate more black income.

Gold inflow is an example of the above argument. During the period that its import was banned (until 1992), approximately 160 tons of gold were smuggled into the country. The amount of gold inflow increased to 900 tons by 1998; of this amount approximately half was smuggled into the country. Thus, the legal imports increased but so did the illegal inflow. This was a consequence of the profit that could be made on smuggled gold since it was also part of the hawala transactions and the smuggling of goods that was taking place. The loss of savings to the country increased 5.5 times. Gold is an unproductive investment since it does not lead to further production as happens when one sets up a plant or a business. Further, since India does not produce enough gold to meet demand, it is imported, and for that savings flow out. The more the investment in gold the more the loss of productive capital to the economy. Also, due to its linkage with other forms of illegality, its flows result in more black income generation.

Just as with gold imports, all across the economic spectrum criminal activity increased. A triad of corrupt politicians, businessmen and the executive which was already in place changed its style of functioning and the way it shared the gains from corruption. Many politicians became businessmen—openly or by setting up proxies who at times were their family members. Businessmen also entered politics in larger numbers. Privatization and the establishment of the infrastructure of the private sector (in public-private partnership mode) offered new opportunities for making illegal gains by cornering resources like land, forests and mines. Greater participation by the private sector since 1991 in the education and health sectors has also created enormous opportunities to indulge in illegalities. As has been mentioned, the number of scams and the amount of money involved per scam has grown exponentially in the decades since then.

The generation of black income involves illegality,

and the available data suggests that illegality has been growing even though crimes are often not registered. Systems have been set up to bribe politicians and the executive for the adulteration of food and medicines, for not declaring the full output produced so that profits are generated off the balance sheet and so on. The working of the market mechanism has not dented these structures.

The increase in the collection of direct taxes as a percentage of the GDP since 1999 is cited as an example of the working of the market mechanism leading to better compliance. But as has been shown in a 2007 Alternative Economic Survey article, the rise in this ratio is not due to a reduction of the black economy through improved compliance with the tax regime but due to the dramatic rise in the income of the corporate sector. So the black economy has continued to grow.

In brief, systematic illegality and corruption in the country has its roots in big business and the triad it helped create so that it could manipulate policy. This has led to the strengthening of organized crime in the country. The problems fostered at the borders with neighbours and the hawala links for flight of capital have enabled the linkage between local illegality and transnational crime to grow. Finally, the indiscriminate opening up of the economy in 1991 has led to a further spread of illegality and crime.

IV

························· ～ ·························

WHAT FUELS THE BLACK ECONOMY?

So far in this book we have attempted to define the black economy, dispelled some of the misconceptions surrounding it, looked at how widespread it is today, surveyed its origins and analysed how it has grown. Given its widespread character and its deleterious impact, it needs to be tackled head on. For that we need to know: what fuels it? In this chapter we will look in some detail at who and what is responsible for the black economy. As always, various misconceptions abound. It is thought that some of the main causes for the existence of the black economy in India are the following:

- Low salaries of the bureaucracy and the police who are to implement the laws.
- High rate of inflation and speculation.
- High tax rates.

- High degree of controls and regulations in society.

Let's look at each of them in turn. Some analysts have suggested that the low salaries of bureaucrats, the police, the judiciary and other law-and-order and regulatory authorities lead to the generation of black incomes. It is thought that because these people are ill paid, there is a drive to make extra money and that leads them to use their position to demand and get bribes. That is certainly the case, but the black income generated because of this is not large. Of the black incomes generated through committing an illegality, bribes often are in the range of 5 to 15 per cent.

The thought underlying this idea is that there is a demonstration effect from the developed nations. Those in power want a lifestyle comparable to that enjoyed by their counterparts in advanced economies. In order to enable this their salaries, it is argued, should be much higher. This does not make sense. How can employees in these sectors be given salaries comparable to those paid in an advanced country when India's per capita income is not even 5 per cent of that in the advanced countries? If even 5 per cent of the population in India is given a salary comparable to that available in the advanced countries, there will be nothing left for the rest of the population. The origin of the problem can be traced to growing consumerism in India.

Further, the salaries currently paid to the bureaucracy and the police are a multiple of India's per capita income, hence they cannot be called low. They are low only in comparison with the salaries of their counterparts in advanced countries. There is another reason why the bureaucracy or the police feel dissatisfied. In any society, there is an income ladder which is historically given and traditionally accepted. Economic theory suggests that when this changes rapidly, disaffection rises. In India, the business class has rapidly increased its income relative to all others and that has led to disaffection. Much of this income is believed by many to be based on committing illegalities of some kind and is resented by those who are left behind. For all the foregoing reasons it would be incorrect to blame low salaries (in absolute terms or in comparison to those in the advanced countries) as a cause of the generation of black incomes.

What about the theory that inflation and speculation lead to black income generation? Inflation and speculation result in higher incomes for businesses, but that cannot by itself be a cause of black income generation. Even after paying taxes honestly, more is left from the higher income earned through speculation than the lower income these people were getting earlier. So, in itself, this cannot be the cause of black income generation.

Extreme speculation, by flouting government regulations, when there are shortages, does result in black income generation since it is associated with an illegality. The cause then is illegality and not speculation. Worthy of more serious consideration are the hypotheses that the high tax rate and a high degree of regulation are responsible for the generation of black income.

IV.1 HIGH TAX RATE HYPOTHESIS

The idea underlying this hypothesis is an obvious one—people do not pay their taxes fully because they find them to be high. The real question to be asked is, what is a high tax rate? This is not easily defined. In some countries like Sweden, in 1985, the highest tax rate was 85 per cent but people did not evade taxes; the black economy there was estimated to be only 1 per cent of GDP.

By and large, around the world, responsible citizens understand that they are being taxed so that these revenues can be used to provide goods and services to society. Of course, there is an administration which enables these goods and services to be made available to the public and therefore there are administrative costs. This expenditure is said to be unproductive but without it the delivery of these public goods is not feasible. It can be more or less efficient and one must strive to move towards greater efficiency. But the cost of administration is an essential cost which cannot be escaped. It is to be found not just in the public sector but in the private sector as well. Witness the massive expenditures incurred by corporate executives to fuel extravagant lifestyles—swanky corporate offices, airplanes, seven-star luxury living and so on. This has become the style in both the public and the private sectors.

Taxes are recycled to the public in the form of public goods and services. In the developed world, which functions more efficiently for the most part, the citizenry feels that it is getting a good return for its taxes as public goods and services work efficiently. In order to pay for this, citizens pay taxes voluntarily and the size of the black economy remains small, as in the case of the Scandinavian economies. A vast majority of the citizens there feel that the high tax they pay comes back to them in the form of quality education, healthcare, clean environment, infrastructure and so on—all the things that enable them to lead a civilized existence.

In developing countries, tax-paying citizens often feel cheated because they see others getting away with paying little or no taxes. Those earning a fixed income see businessmen and self-employed professionals getting away with paying little taxes. Further, they see money wasted by governments and negligible benefits accruing to them. They see the government and corporates squandering money. They hear of corruption in high and low places and feel aggrieved. This results in a widespread sense of social injustice and that weakens the commitment to paying taxes. The problem then is not high or low taxes, but the citizen's sense of belonging to society.

Be that as it may, what has the situation been in India? Are Indian taxes high? Indeed, in 1971, when Mrs Gandhi was the prime minister and the finance minister, the highest tax rate was 97.5 per cent. For incomes above ₹15 lakh the tax rate became 102 per cent since there was also a wealth tax. As a result, no one could have an annual income above ₹15 lakh. At that time the Wanchoo Committee had estimated the size of the black economy to be 7 per cent of GDP. Tax rates since then have come down systematically and are now at 30 per cent (plus some surcharges) but the size of the black economy has gone up to 62 per cent.

From the mid-1970s to the mid-1990s, the sum that India used to collect from direct taxes was between 2.5 per cent and 2.7 per cent of GDP. This was in spite of the lowering of income tax rates. This figure started rising when new schemes (called, one for five and one for six) were introduced to bring more people into the tax net. These schemes required one to file a tax return if one belonged to one of the five or six categories (if one went abroad or was a member of a club and so on). Roughly one per cent of Indians used to pay income tax till the end of the 1990s. Today, the direct tax-GDP ratio has risen to about 5.5 per cent. The number of people in the tax net has gone up to about 52 million from around 12 million in the late 1990s. Has this success been the result of the lowering of tax rates? Not really.

What has happened is that the government's policies are based on 'growth at any cost'. As a result, inequalities have risen dramatically from the end of the 1990s. Thus, those in the higher tax brackets are earning a lot more and, therefore, paying more taxes on their declared incomes. But they are also generating a lot of black income. For instance, after 1992, when the cap on managerial salaries at ₹3,12,000 was removed, salaries soared and by the 2000s there were many top executives earning crores of rupees. At the same time, the minimum daily wage was ₹35 in the 1990s; this had risen to ₹105 by the mid-2000s. So, the minimum wage rose by a factor of 3 while managerial salaries jumped by a factor of 100. Corporate profits also soared, but because compliance did not improve, more black incomes were generated rather than less.

A 2007 Alternative Economic Survey article showed

that the rise in the direct tax to GDP ratio was a result of increase in inequality and not better compliance. A 2016 *Economic and Political Weekly* article shows that even though the number of people in the direct tax net has risen to 52 million in 2012-2013, the latest year for which the data was released (from 1999 to 2015 the government did not release this data), the effective number of taxpayers was approximately 15 million or just about 1.2 per cent of the population. Thus, the tax base has not broadened effectively in spite of lower tax rates.

Similarly, in the case of indirect taxes, the rates have come down, especially after 1991. The peak customs duties used to be 320 per cent and the average used to be around 150 per cent. These have come down to an average of 15 per cent. Yet, black income generation and the flight of capital via under- and over-invoicing not only continues but has grown.

A National Institute of Public Finance and Policy (NIPFP) 1985 publication showed that in the case of the sugar industry, even though excise duties changed between 1962 and 1980, there was no correlation between this and the black incomes generated in this industry. In the case of sales tax, the government offered a low tax (about 2 per cent of their income) to the traders to make them come into the tax net, but this scheme did not meet with any success. So, in spite of lowering of indirect tax rates, compliance in these taxes did not improve.

In brief, the evasion of taxes, whether direct or indirect, is not linked to the rates of taxes alone.

IV.2 CONTROLS: CAN A LAW BE ITS OWN CAUSE OF VIOLATION?

It has been argued that the licence-permit-quota raj or the inspector raj has been one of the important causes for black income generation by businesses. It is argued that the officialdom in charge of the implementation of laws pertaining to businesses makes an extra buck by allowing businesses to flout the relevant laws. For instance, if labour laws, like safety precautions, are flouted, then an extra income can be generated by the business. Similarly, if a food-processing concern on the banks of a river discharges its effluents directly into the river without treatment, it is able to save costs and thereby increase its income. To commit these illegalities, all the management needs to do is to bribe the inspector who comes to check. The cause then is neither the inspectors coming to check the proper implementation of laws nor the laws themselves which they are supposed to enforce.

Controls and regulations have a history. They come up in response to social needs. For instance, as mentioned earlier, during World War II, rents soared and people could not afford them. In response to the situation, rent control was imposed. This continued on the statute books long after the situation normalized. Once a law is passed, it is often difficult to repeal it since vested interests build around it. Certain laws need to be repealed when they are no longer required; however, there cannot be a general prescription that all controls and regulations be removed.

Positing that controls and regulations are responsible for the generation of black incomes is like saying that a law is its own cause of violation. Let us say that a traffic light is installed at a busy intersection to regulate traffic. It cannot be said that the existence of the traffic light leads to people jumping traffic lights. The traffic light serves a social purpose, namely regulating traffic. Eliminating it would get rid of the problem of people jumping the light but it would lead to perpetual chaos at the intersection. When the traffic density increases, traffic lights cannot help and flyovers and underpasses are built. The problem of people ignoring traffic lights also gets mitigated to some extent but traffic lights cannot be done away with altogether. It also points to the fact that as society becomes more complex, new situations arise and different forms of regulation and controls are needed.

When environmental regulations are flouted, can it be said that they are not needed and should be eliminated? Or that building and zoning laws in a city are redundant? Clearly, they are needed, and it is the corruption around their enforcement that needs to be eliminated rather than eliminating the controls. These laws are not responsible for their violation. It is the drive of the businesses to make an extra profit over and above what they can make by following rules that is at the root of the problem. The cause then is the illegality that is committed in an activity and not the law itself, which only prescribes the rules by which the activity is to be conducted.

People have argued for free markets; they would like laws and rules to be eliminated. But it needs to be remembered that rules define the way we govern ourselves; that is how we structure our society. There is nothing like a free market. All markets function by implicit or explicit rules enforced by law as administered by the state. When we take a taxi, it is implicitly understood that the taxi driver will not overcharge and will take the shortest possible route to the destination. There is no contract signed at the start of a journey, but there is the implicit authority of the state to enforce this rule. Society is full of such understandings and these are enforced by the responsible behaviour of all citizens.

The state cannot be present everywhere. But without the state there would be chaos and a free-for-all. The more powerful will enforce their will and jungle raj will ensue.

IV.2.1 Less Government, Not No Rules

As societies have become more complex, cases of market failure have increased. Economic theory suggests that when market-driven solutions fail, the government has to intervene to enable society to reach the most desirable (optimum) situation for it. For example, in India the girl child is not given the same priority in education or health as the male child, because of the tradition that after marriage she will leave. But this is sub-optimal for society since she is responsible for the health and education of the child. If her health and education levels were better, that would mean her children would be better off too. So, left to the markets, the situation would not be a desirable one for society. The government has to intervene and improve the situation for the girl child through the creation of special provisions, schemes and programmes. Similarly, in the case of sanitation and sewage, government intervention is required in order to make cities cleaner and hygienic.

Yes, there should be the least possible government in societies but not necessarily an absence of rules and regulations. If citizens automatically follow rules and regulations we would need less state apparatus and regulatory authorities, and overt regulation could be minimized. The more the rules are flouted, the more the regulatory apparatus and costs of enforcement and less the efficiency.

In India, the elites appear to be lawless. It could be said of them that they regard being in power as not just giving them the authority to enforce the rules but also the capacity to bestow favours, often involving a quid pro quo. The attitude is feudal—one can exploit one's position. From the lowest to the highest, the elite tend to flout rules. From infractions as small as jumping traffic lights to bigger ones like violating environmental regulations, building by-laws or zoning by-laws. Can cities survive without building or zoning by-laws? How can city planning be done without some norms? No wonder then that in India, cities are characterized by the breakdown of urban infrastructure, unhygienic conditions, disease and large-scale pollution. Even where the private sector has set up posh townships, adequate facilities are lacking because the developer has flouted rules to make an extra buck. Those who buy property from such developers then suffer the consequences for a long time.

In India, laws on paper are very good but their

implementation is weak. Instead of trying to implement them better, the laws themselves are changed from time to time via amendments or by executive order. This makes the laws more complex but does not guarantee that they will be followed. Greater complexity makes it difficult to implement the rules and, therefore, it becomes easier to flout them. Income tax rules are an obvious case in point. The 1960 Income Tax Act was a simple one. As people found more loopholes to avoid tax payments, the department formulated new rules to plug them. This made the rules more and more complex and more difficult for the officers to implement.

Thus, it is essential that there be a consensus on rules and regulations so that the citizens automatically follow them, especially the elite. In a divided society, achieving consensus is difficult but there is no escaping it. Less government should not mean less rules but better enforced rules. So, in India, the problem is not that there are too many rules and regulations but that every single rule is violated by a lawless elite and enforcement is very weak.

IV.3 THE TRIAD

The black economy is growing in spite of the reduction in tax rates since 1971 and the whittling away of controls and regulation in the economy over the last three decades. This is not surprising since these are not the causes of generation of black incomes.

To effectively tackle the black economy there is a need to identify the correct cause(s) underlying its existence and growth. For the black economy to constitute 62 per cent of GDP as it does at present, the reasons for its thriving would need to be both 'systematic and systemic'. In practice, it works as a system just like the white economy functions as a system. This is only possible if those in charge of monitoring and the implementation of rules are a party to black income generation. They have to connive in the persistence of illegality and share the extra profits generated. Thus, a triad of corrupt businessmen, politicians and executive emerges to drive the black economy.

IV.3.1 Examples From Day-to-Day Life

In a Delhi Development Authority (DDA) colony, set up by the government, when construction work begins on an illegal addition or extension to an existing building, the local safai karamchari (or street cleaner) informs the local beat constable, the DDA and municipal officials in charge of the area. Soon these worthies come to the site and settle the amount of money they will charge to overlook the new construction. Later, the property tax man comes and demands his share to manipulate the property tax rate in favour of those constructing the structure. Everyone gets a share of the extra economic benefit the owner of the property stands to make.

To take another example, in Delhi, the height of private homes is restricted to two and a half storeys. There are also regulations that govern the built-up area of houses, i.e. a certain amount of land on which the building stands needs to remain empty. However, most buildings flout these restrictions. The only way this could happen is if there is a concerted effort to bypass the rules by all those responsible for adhering to or enforcing them, starting with the architect who has to draw up the plans and get them approved. It is little surprise, therefore, that in a city like Delhi, or any other city in the country, for that matter, most buildings flout rules and restrictions.

Encroachment on vacant land owned by the state, (including pavements and roads) is widespread. Here again the official machinery and the local politician are a party to allowing this to happen. Slum clusters appear with the connivance of the developers, local politicians and the department in charge of the land parcel. A weekly/monthly payment (hafta) is extracted from the encroachers. Traders, pavement stall owners and rehri sellers (street hawkers) all have to pay hafta to various officials for carrying on their trade. One cannot encroach upon even a square yard of land without paying hafta.

In production, as we have seen, under- and over-invoicing takes place in a systematic way. The accounts department, the official machinery (like excise and sales tax officials), the police, the inspectors, trade channels are all involved in this manipulation. Once these channels are set up, the tax rate becomes immaterial, and the business is assured of a certain return whether the tax rate is 97 per cent or 30 per cent.

Similar examples can be given from the construction industry, foreign trade, various service industries and so on. The point is that rules and laws are systematically violated and those in charge of maintaining the law of the land profit from such violations.

IV.3.2 Criminals in the Nexus

A triad of corrupt businessmen, corrupt politicians and corrupt members of the executive is formed for the purpose of systematically circumventing the law. The corrupt members of the executive are drawn from the police, bureaucracy and judiciary. Since the 1980s criminals have become part of the equation. Either the businessman or the politician has a criminal record.

An amnesty was given to smugglers in 1983 so that they could be brought into the mainstream. But this led to the entry of criminals into politics, or at least their more active participation in politics. Prior to this, they had financed politicians but remained largely in the background. As criminals entered the legislatures, the rule of law weakened. They influenced the police, the bureaucracy and the judiciary to ensure decisions went in their favour and also interfered more blatantly in decision-making.

Today, the triad has grown so powerful that even an incorruptible head of government is often powerless to control it. The black economy continues to prosper and there is growing criminalization in society. Ironically, a clean head of the government serves a useful role for the triad to survive and prosper because she/he provides credibility for a largely corrupt system—a mascot. It helps keep the public confused about the real nature of the power structure.

The triad is of benefit to all its elements. Businessmen are able to influence policy and protect their ill-gotten profits. The other two constituents of the triad need the businessmen to invest their funds and launder them. There is hardly much point in keeping the money under the mattress or in a locker when it can earn a return. Most politicians have at least one businessman close to them who provides such services.

IV.3.3 Media in the Nexus

Of late, some powerful media persons have become party to these illegalities, as their companies benefit from the association. Sometimes, these media persons play the role of the middleman in parleys between businessmen, politicians and the executive, as evidenced by the Radia Tapes exposé.

The corruption of the media goes back quite a long way and is most apparent during elections. Politicians and parties need positive publicity and must avoid adverse publicity. For this they have been paying the local press per column centimetre for positive coverage. The Press Council of India published a report in 2010 on this phenomenon, now called 'paid news', highlighting its prevalence and pointing out that it was a threat to the freedom of the press. The tragedy is that media is being increasingly manipulated by corporations, politicians and the executive; today, a substantial percentage of the media has turned into a PR machine, not an independent pillar of a democratic state. The manipulation of the press has become even more blatant of late with big companies owning some of the country's biggest media organizations. The only saving grace is that because of the proliferation of media channels and national dailies, there is competition to come out with exposés and there are still some organizations which expose scams and provide some checks on the triad and its power.

IV.3.4 *The Future*

Any number of steps have been taken to control the growth of the black economy but they have failed because the triad has grown stronger. It is not the availability of laws that is the problem but their lax implementation. Also, the dynamism and 'flexibility' of the triad is such that the ways in which black income is accumulated keeps pace with changes in the laws. Any law should be a law both in practice and in spirit. There is no perfect law, however good it may appear on paper. If the spirit is not willing, human ingenuity finds ways around it sooner than later.

One can see that in India, for a long time, defection from political parties has been sought to be curbed so that the cynical manipulation of politicians for money or power can be prevented. However, legislators have found ways around each of the laws put in place. Instead of individual legislators defecting, groups of them started switching sides; eventually most of the (or even the entire) legislative group have resorted to change in its allegiance. In sum, the existence of the triad is the main reason the black economy continues to flourish in India. Businessmen and traders belonging to the triad are the biggest culprits where tax evasion is concerned, in connivance with the executive and the political class. It is this nexus that enables the country's controls and regulations to be violated systematically. The common man is helpless in the face of this powerful nexus. Its existence is the single biggest reason why the development of India is stunted.

V

REMEDIES

Dozens of committees, commissions and parliamentary committees have gone into different aspects of the black economy and have suggested thousands of measures to control it. So we are not short of suggestions or of measures to tackle the problem. Among the suggestions that have been made are voluntary disclosure schemes, demonetization, payment by cheque or online banking, and so on and so forth. Some of these steps have not only not helped curb the menace but have in fact fuelled it because they have added to the complexity of the laws or turned people into habitual law breakers. More importantly, they have not gone to the heart of the problem. As we have seen, the cause of the growing illegality lies in the desire of the elite to make incomes over and above what they can make legally.

Broadly, most of the reports have opined that the phenomenon of black economy is related to the government. Hence, in one form or the other, their recommendations are based on a scaling down (or elimination) of government intervention in the economy. As discussed earlier, the underlying cause is the triad, which implies a joint product of the public and private sectors. Thus any remedy has to be based on the dismantling of the triad. Even if one component of the triad is eliminated, the black economy would begin to collapse.

In this chapter I would like to appraise a number of schemes that have been tried (including Modi's demonetization scheme). I will also provide brief outlines of remedies that can be tried in the short, medium and long term to eradicate or at least substantially reduce the problem.

V.1 WHAT HAS NOT WORKED

V.1.1 Voluntary Disclosure Schemes

As discussed in Chapter IV, even though tax rates and controls have been drastically reduced in India, the black economy has continued to flourish. It has been argued that if the black savings accumulated over time could be channelled into the white economy then at least it could contribute to the development of the economy. This was the idea behind the government announcing the Voluntary Disclosure Schemes, which were introduced six times until 1997. The government also came out with a Bearer Bond Scheme in 1979-1980. In 2016 it floated an Income Declaration Scheme. The idea underlying these latter two schemes was also to raise resources for development.

Unfortunately, all of these schemes proved to be counter-productive. The Comptroller and Auditor General (CAG) Report on the 1997 scheme, for example, said that it had made people habitual tax offenders. Many people declared their incomes in the earlier schemes and then again in 1997. The reason is obvious—people begin to expect that such schemes will come along from time to time so they feel they can generate black incomes today and whiten them tomorrow when the next such scheme is floated. The CAG report further argued that the honest taxpayer felt cheated since they had paid their taxes honestly while the dishonest fellow who had not paid taxes was getting off lightly. Consequently, such people also tend to turn dishonest and more black income generation takes place.

The ineffectiveness of these kinds of schemes shows a lack of imagination on the part of government as well as an inability to come to grips with the problem for a variety of reasons that I have explored throughout the book. This is not a good thing at all. It emboldens those who make black income, as they feel they can get away with their crime. It makes the state appear weak and this has all sorts of social and political consequences.

V.1.2 Acquisition of Undervalued Real Estate

Real estate, though not a generator of black income, leads to its circulation and, therefore, to ease of generation. In that sense it is important for black income generation. In real estate, a part of the purchase price is in white and the rest is in black. Very often the ratio is 60:40 but it varies depending on the type of property, location and so on. So, typically, the price of property registered is much less than the actual transaction price. The government loses tax on the capital gains. The state and local government lose on stamp duty, transfer charges and property tax. No wonder, in spite of the massive development of real estate in the country, municipal corporations are always short of resources for local development. These bodies are supposed to provide civic infrastructure, but due to lack of adequate resources the quality of civic amenities is poor and the urban infrastructure in most Indian cities is crumbling.

To check the under-valuation of property the government introduced a scheme for the acquisition of undervalued property. The government could offer a 15 per cent higher price than the one declared in a transaction and acquire the property; it was felt that the property could later be auctioned at close to its true market price. This was supposed to act as a deterrent to undervaluation since the individual would lose the value of their property. Unfortunately, this did not prove to be a deterrent and the undervaluation continued.

A nexus emerged between the property valuer, the income tax officer in-charge and the seller. For a consideration, the under-valuation was accepted. Things were arranged in such a manner that all transactions would take place at a similar undervaluation so the officer could not officially show that there was undervaluation in any particular transaction. However, in interviews, it became clear that the officers knew the price of each transaction since that was necessary to figure out the amount of the bribe they could collect from the transaction.

It also needs to be kept in mind that the income tax department is not able to audit more than a small percentage of the accounts where returns are filed. As the number of returns has increased the percentage that can be audited has dropped. Thus, dealing with a large number of annual sales transactions is not feasible for the income tax department. So, though in theory the idea of acquisition of undervalued property was good, in practice it did not work out.

V.1.3 Technology-related Solutions

It is often thought that technology can be used to solve the problem of black income generation. For example, it is said that the advent of mobile phones has reduced the importance of telephone linesmen. In India, during the era of fixed landlines (before 1997, after which mobile phones became affordable), telephones used to go out of order frequently. Each time this happened, one was dependent on the linesman to come and find the fault and repair the line/instrument. For this, one had to keep the linesmen happy by giving them a tip. It has therefore been argued that thanks to the new technology the importance of the linesmen, and therefore the need to tip them, has reduced. However, the corruption in the auction of the spectrum far exceeded what the linesmen would have earned in thirty years. Similarly, with the coming of the internet, the telegraph man has become insignificant. One used to give him a tip but now that the telegraph itself has become obsolete, no tip is needed. Now one uses emails for instant communication and new forms of electronic fraud have emerged.

To take another example of this kind of thinking, it was felt that the allotment of a Permanent Account Number (PAN) to each income taxpayer would reduce black income generation since it would help in collating all the income of individual taxpayers. However, this has not helped since corrupt tax evaders have started keeping multiple PAN accounts and found a way around the electronic (computerized) aspect by misspelling names and addresses to create more accounts. It is also not easy to keep track of all the financial information on a person because of the various devices available to hide the trail of money flows, like the use of hawala or front companies, or round tripping (the return of capital that was earlier sent abroad). Use of front companies implies opening companies in the names of others and using them to route one's transactions so that they are not traceable to the original source. Moreover, as we have seen, the tax department is not equipped to audit a large number of cases annually.

The reason virtually all the schemes that have been floated in the past have failed to work is because they have not attacked the core of the problem—the corrupt triad that enables and fosters the black economy. No government has shown the necessary guts and will to tackle corrupt big businessmen, corrupt members of the executive and corrupt political leaders, especially those belonging to their own parties, without which the problem of the black economy will never be solved. A good example of a well-intentioned scheme that will not have much of an effect in curbing the black economy is Modi's recent demonetization scheme that needlessly created great hardship for many millions and disrupted the economic momentum the country had succeeded in building up. Let us analyse it in some detail.

V:2.1 Modi's Demonetization

When the government announced the demonetization of all ₹500 and ₹1,000 notes in November 2016, it said it was doing so for two reasons—it wanted to eliminate counterfeit currency used by terrorists and smugglers, and it wanted to destroy the black economy by forcing the 'de-hoarding' of cash held by those generating black income.

The objectives of the government were laudable, but it seems as though the scheme was imposed on the country with little or no forethought. First, it must be understood that the black money the government was targeting is only about 1 per cent of the black wealth held in the country and only 3.5 per cent of the black income generated in 2016. Even if the government managed to suck out all the black cash in circulation, it would not have much effect on the black economy which involves various activities in which black incomes are generated. It does not stop these activities from continuing. Moreover, 80 per cent of the ₹500 and ₹1,000 notes (which constituted 86 per cent of the cash in circulation) was not black money, but rather white money used by businesses and citizens. Not only do a vast majority of Indians, rich and poor, use cash and not credit cards for daily financial transactions but businesses need it for working capital to buy raw materials, pay wages and other requirements for production and sales.

Making the situation worse was the inept execution of the demonetization scheme. If over 85 per cent of a country's currency is demonetized at one go, replacing it will take months if not years. The capacity to print notes is limited, especially if smaller denomination notes are required. ATMs had to be reconfigured to take in the new notes (as they were of different dimensions than the ones they were replacing) and this apparently was not thought of and took much longer than anticipated. I will not go into the sloppiness of execution as this has been widely discussed in great detail. What I would like to point out is the fallacious thinking behind the scheme, including factors such as the following:

- Only a small amount of the black economy would be

affected by the demonetization. We have seen why.

- Much of the money that was demonetized was not black cash.

- According to the Pew Research Centre, in 2015, only 22 per cent of adults in India had access to the internet. This means the vast majority who do not have access to the internet will be unable to use online banking.

- Only 17 per cent of Indians have access to smart phones and consequently to mobile phone banking.

- In a population of 1.3 billion and counting, there are 24.5 million credit cards and 661.8 million debit cards. A fairly large number of Indians do not have access to credit or debit cards. Most small business do not have card readers so the cashless economy the prime minister and his cheerleaders have been talking of cannot become a reality overnight.

- It is unlikely that black marketeers and other generators of black money will suffer because the biggest fish were able to quickly convert whatever black cash they had into white. Some of the avenues used, according to media reports, were the purchase of jewellery, cash donations to temples, conversion of old notes to new notes with the connivance of corrupt bank officials and circulation through the Jan Dhan accounts of the poor. In other words, despite the massive exercise of demonetization, the total amount of black cash that has been demobilized is very small.

• It was not explained why when high currency notes were being demonetized—as they were the choice of currency for black income generators to hoard—currency of even higher denomination (the ₹2,000 note) was being introduced. Surely, this would be even easier to hoard?

• Further, it was thought that the scheme would nullify the counterfeit currency which is thought to be used to finance terrorist activity. However, what doesn't seem to have been taken into account is that each counterfeit note can only be used by a terrorist once to finance terrorist activity; counterfeit currency is therefore constantly being generated and the one-time extinguishing of counterfeit currency does not solve the problem. Moreover, if the old notes could be counterfeited it is likely that the same will happen to the new notes. It must also be understood that terrorist activity is not just financed with Indian currency, it can be and is fuelled by dollars, gold, diamonds, drugs and so on. Terrorism is a continuing problem, not a one-off thing.

In sum, the demonetization scheme will not solve the

problem of the black economy. However, the economy has been hit. The livelihoods of the poor and small traders who depend overwhelmingly on cash have been especially hit hard. They have had to reduce their expenditures, leading to decline in demand across the economy. The well-off sections facing uncertainty have also cut back discretionary expenditure on things like white goods. All this has impacted agriculture, services and industry. As the profits of industries decline, they may not be able to pay their loans soon so that the NPAs (non-performing assets) in banks will rise. As a result of this, the capacity of the banks to lend will decline further. Businesses facing excess capacity and uncertainty have cut back investment.

Thus, since demonetization was announced, unemployment has risen, investment has fallen, banks are facing difficulties and the crisis in agriculture has been aggravated in spite of a good monsoon. All this leads to the emergence of recessionary conditions in the economy.

The notion that if a few lakh crores of old notes do not return to the banks, it will somehow become available to the government which it can spend on schemes for the poor is unlikely to be realized since, according to reports, most of the old notes seem to have been returned.

It was also believed that when banks become flush

with funds they could give these out as loans. It was argued that interest rates could be lowered so as to boost investment. But as soon as enough cash is available people will withdraw their money. So, this is a temporary deposit and can only be seen as short-term lending. Further, to begin with, the bankers were too busy dealing with cash to focus on lending. Regarding lower interest rates leading to an increase in investment, this is unlikely to take place since when capacity utilization is low, investments do not take place. In the US, Eurozone, etc., in spite of interest rates being close to zero, investment did not revive for a long time after the 2007 economic meltdown.

It has been argued that the budget could stand to benefit through increased tax collection as the black economy declines. However, as argued, the black economy is unlikely to be impacted by demonetization. Even if there is an effect, it will be small. The bigger impact is likely to be the advent of recessionary conditions and a decline in production and incomes which will adversely affect tax collection, leading to an increase in deficit and additional problems for the government.

There could be a benefit over the medium term. The organized sector and some sections of the unorganized sector may move towards using less cash. The government is pushing hard for it and so are the companies involved in electronic banking and related financial companies.

Even though all this will take time, it could help make the economy more efficient in the medium run. The proponents of this move expect that people using electronic transfers of money will leave a trail which will make it more difficult to generate black incomes. If this comes about, the demonetization would have been of some use, but all this lies in the future and there is no guarantee that it will happen. Moreover, this move could have been initiated independently of demonetization and with adequate preparation.

In brief, the demonetization scheme has had deleterious short, mid-term and long-term effects. Meanwhile, illegal activities, black markets and real estate scams, the production of spurious drugs, capitation fees and various other components of the black economy will carry on after a brief hiatus.

V.2.2 *Other Recent Steps*

The NDA government came to power in 2014 on the promise of checking the growing black economy. In an election promise, the BJP claimed that there was a lot of black money abroad and that it would be easy to bring it back. Not only that, it was said that there would be enough to give each family ₹15 lakh. The Opposition has been taunting the ruling party about this promise which remains unfulfilled. At the same time, the government has done little about the Vyapam Scam and the other ongoing investigations of scams.

In 2014 we saw the setting up of the Supreme Court-ordered Special Investigation Team (SIT). The SIT has submitted five reports but these have not been made public so nothing much is known about what the recommendations are and whether they are implementable.

A very tough sounding law, the Black Money (Undisclosed Foreign Income and Assets) and Imposition of Tax Act, was passed in 2015 and was supposed to induce people to bring back black wealth stashed away abroad. According to reports, this measure resulted in a little over 600 declarations and over ₹2,000 crore in tax being collected. Since the amount held abroad may be in lakhs of crores of rupees not even 1 per cent of the illicit funds taken out of the country since 1948 has been disclosed under this scheme. The reason is simple—people who have funds abroad know that the government has not been able to track them or trace their wealth over the last seventy years and the new bill does not have any provision by which they can be tracked. So they have little to worry about.

An Income Declaration Scheme (IDS) was announced in the 2016-2017 budget. It was open from 1 June to 30

September 2016, during which time 64,275 people came forward to declare ₹65,250 crore of black money. No doubt, this is the largest amount of declaration of black money in the history of Indian taxation. The average amount of black income per declaration was about one crore rupees. As we have seen, the current size of the black economy is estimated to be 62 per cent of GDP (or, at current prices, about ₹93 lakh crore in 2016-2017). Thus, what has been declared is roughly 0.7 per cent of the black income generation in the year. In the 1997 scheme, what was declared was roughly 5 per cent of the black income generated in that year. The number of declarations in 1997 was over four lakh while now, surprisingly, it is a sixth of this number.

The government's own efforts at tracking black income generators who have stashed their illicit funds abroad have yielded little results. In this regard, the government has been extolling the virtues of Double Taxation Avoidance Agreements (DTAA) with close to ninety countries and its Tax Information Exchange (TIE) agreements with around thirty-five countries. It has made out a case that these agreements will enable the tax department to catch those with black wealth abroad.

However, in spite of numerous DTAA signed in the last twenty-seven years, hardly anyone is known to have been brought to book under this provision. In reality,

DTAA ensures that the declared income is not taxed in two countries. It is not about the undeclared income. However, it has led to collateral damage by providing the route for round tripping from Mauritius so that black money spirited out could return via that country. At one point, 40 per cent of foreign investment was coming via this jurisdiction.

The treaty with Mauritius has been modified recently to discourage round tripping by making a provision for the taxation of capital gains. But, apparently, new avenues have been created to allow this activity to continue. The treaties with Cayman Islands and Singapore are also in the process of being modified. In spite of all these treaties and earlier provisions to check the outflow of illicit funds from India, data suggests that illicit flows from the country have increased since 1991.

These illicit flows are facilitated by hawala operations big and small. Even well-known banks have been accused of running hawala operations, and it is imperative that the authorities act swiftly against anyone accused of facilitating the outflow of illicit funds.

There is a need to end banking secrecy but India has not done so. It was alleged that a high-profile foreign banking corporation was involved in the Hasan Ali case but the bank has not faced prosecution. Businesses can have secrecy about their business but not about incomes which is a public issue because of taxation. Similarly, banks should not be allowed secrecy about deposits and depositors.

In brief, the government's recent steps have not yielded results on the control of the black economy.

V.3 WHAT MAY WORK

As I've emphasized throughout the book, in order to tackle the black economy, the triad of corrupt politicians, businessmen and the executive has to be dismantled. Even if one of these three wings is undermined, the triad will collapse. This can only be done via changes in the politics of the land. It cannot be achieved by the good intentions of someone or by some technical devices.

One needs to think of the remedies in the long, medium and short term. In the long run, one will have to go for structural changes relating to the economy and society as a whole. The executive will need to be overhauled, the regulation of corporates and business in general will need to be redone, and political reforms will have to be carried out. In the medium term, given the structural changes, there has to be the targeting of changes in sectoral policies, especially in areas like real estate, and imaginative and simplified tax policies. Short-term changes will require implementation of policies that are already in place. Unquestionably, the inadequacies of existing structures and manipulation of monitoring and regulatory infrastructures will make them of limited use. But there is an immediate requirement for laws that can eliminate hawala and banking secrecy as well as rigorous implementation of schemes like the Lokpal and the strengthening of the Right to Information (RTI) Act.

V.3.1 *The Short, Medium and Long Term*

Some policies and ideas that could be implemented are given below:

SHORT TERM

Right to Information

The black economy functions in secrecy. Hence the most important tool that we have, to bring it out into the open is the RTI provision. It is required to bring about transparency and accountability at all levels of societal functioning. It is crucial to bring under RTI all political parties, the judiciary, the prime minister and chief minister's offices. If it is extended to them, it would make the politician and the executive accountable and their functioning transparent so that, unlike at present, they cannot subvert the law deliberately. A bill was passed in 2005 but the present dispensation on Right to Information is proving to be inadequate since a) ways to circumvent it are being found, like flatly denying that information is available, b) important offices (like the prime minister or the judiciary) have been left out of its ambit, c) the whistleblowers who reveal information are being threatened and/or killed, and d) it is far too complex for the common man to use.

The mindset of the politicians and the bureaucracy needs to change for RTI to become effective. That is possible only if information is automatically made available to the public rather than only when demanded.

Action Needed on Available Information and Existing Laws

The government collects a vast amount of information on all kinds of activities of the members of the triad but it is usually kept secret and not acted upon. At times this information is used to politically blackmail or take political advantage. That is why the Opposition cries foul when the government acts against the corrupt. The general public also becomes sceptical of such action.

For instance, information is collected on hawala operators and banking operations but it is not acted on. Recent cases highlighting the misuse of banking secrecy laws have come to light; this has to be stopped. A Lokpal Bill was passed but a Lokpal is yet to be appointed. It is needed to make the executive and the political class accountable. But it must only be implemented for the top echelons. It cannot be for the entire bureaucracy since that would require the creation of another bureaucracy which can also get corrupted.

Who will prevent the Lokpal from getting corrupted? The Philippines has functioned with an ombudsman who is unable to check corruption in high places. If Justice Ramaswamy could be in the dock and the Chief Justice of the Punjab High Court had to take steps against other judges, what is the chance that the highest levels of the judiciary and the executive will not be corrupted or silenced? After initial euphoria, what has the Central Vigilance Commission (CVC) achieved? In other words, *mere formalism will not work.*

Often, at present, penalties on illegal activities are not enforced. There needs to be stricter implementation of these so as to create deterrence. Currently, at the initial stage of investigation, many cases against the powerful are deliberately mismanaged with the result that they go scot-free in the courts. This will change only if the investigative agencies are made accountable and autonomous of political interference, as discussed below. Only if this is done can we create an environment of real deterrence. For instance, corrupt businessmen can be blacklisted by banks and loans denied to them; they should also be speedily prosecuted by the courts.

Autonomy to Institutions

In India, there is no dearth of regulatory authorities but we need to understand why they do not deliver. It is as a result of political interference and this needs to be remedied by giving them greater autonomy but also demanding accountability from them. The selection of the head of the regulatory authorities and the watchdog agencies—CVC, Central Bureau of Investigation (CBI), Enforcement Directorate (ED), Intelligence Bureau (IB), Research and Analysis Wing (RAW), etc.—Public Sector undertakings (PSUs) and banks should be made independent of political bosses and specific ministries. Their accountability should be to Parliament and its committees, as in the case of CAG.

MEDIUM TERM

Changes in the Structure of Taxes

The tax structure needs simplification and modification. In a document brought out in 1994, I suggested many changes which remain valid till date. For example, there should be wealth taxation on all forms of wealth, gift tax and estate duty. This is like the tail wagging the dog. It would force individuals to reveal their income to pay taxes. Corporation tax should be on gross profit and not net so that the costs incurred cannot be manipulated to show lower incomes. Property taxation, which is currently manipulated by fudging the value declared, should be based on site and services valuation. Above all, there is need for simplification of taxation by the elimination of deductions and concessions.

Indirect taxes too need to be simplified by levying them only on final and luxury goods. Once direct tax reform goes through, much more will get collected through this form of taxation so the need for indirect taxes will decline. This would then help in simplifying indirect taxes and eliminating them on basic and essential goods.

In the case of taxation of services, incomes are manipulated since norms are difficult to establish. For instance, how much fees should a doctor or a lawyer charge? Such manipulation of income by those in the services sector needs to be checked via what is called a presumptive tax. Such a tax would be based on the norms of incomes earned by such businesses/professionals. Gross profit taxation would also help prevent the manipulation of incomes in the services sector. It needs to be remembered that this is now the largest sector of the economy and, if tackled effectively, will yield a large amount of tax.

Changes in Laws

Just as changes in the taxation laws are required, other laws will also need to be changed and modified. The Law Commission has been producing reports on the changes required. Many laws are relics of the colonial era and need to be changed to suit the requirements of an independent country. Such analysis of various laws needs to continue but with speed and urgency so as to curb new forms of illegality that are constantly emerging—for instance, with respect to the adoption of new technologies in the financial sector or with regard to internet fraud. There is also the need to plug loopholes wherever they are found. But, as in the case of taxation, they should be simplified for easier implementation and also so that the public can understand them and demand their stricter implementation.

Reform of the Executive

The executive, consisting of the bureaucracy, the police and the judiciary, is in urgent need of reform so that its members truly become public servants rather than lording it over the public. They should be answerable not only to their political bosses but also held accountable to the masses. All public dealings, including in the justice system, need to be time-bound. The citizen should know in how much time action will be forthcoming and there should be accountability for delays. Special favours to those in power will need to be checked since that leads to manipulation by the powerful and delays for ordinary citizens.

Take, for example, the necessary reform of the judiciary. Cases have to be speeded up which requires simplification of court procedures. Things like the notarizing of documents can be done away with since this only adds to the red tape and anything can be notarized. Witness protection is crucial and fake witnesses need to be dealt with severely. With more than thirty million cases pending in courts, the powerful manipulate the system for their own ends and the citizens' faith in justice is eroded. There is neither a shortage of judges nor of courts. The problem is that the judiciary is slow to act and is unaccountable to the public. Cases that should be wound up in six months can take more than six years to be concluded thus clogging the courts and there is no one to question this delay.

India Should Push for Meaningful Global Action

There is pressure globally to check corruption. After 9/11, the US has been pushing to curb terrorist financing and hawala. Post the global financial crisis the US realized that it was losing $100 billion of taxes via Base Erosion Profit Shifting (BEPS) and tax havens. So, along with the Organisation for Economic Co-operation and Development (OECD) it has been battling these features of the global financial architecture. However, the fight remains incomplete because many of the OECD countries are either tax havens or have a part of their territory as tax havens. For instance, Delaware in the US and London in the UK provide facilities to financial institutions, which enable them to manipulate the financial system to their advantage. The global financial architecture is to blame for much of the flight of capital from the developing world, including India. This is in need of urgent reform.

To check the flight of capital there is need for the creation of global databases on companies and their trade. Intra-firm MNC trade is at the root of much flight of capital via BEPS and transfer pricing. A global database can check this by providing the data on nation by nation earnings of each subsidiary of an MNC. Partner country data on trade (like the data collected by the International

Monetary Fund called the direction of trade (DOT) data) can check transfer pricing. The United Nations convention on corruption is stronger than the provisions incorporated in the DTAA. These should supersede the DTAA provisions for stricter implementation of data sharing among nations. Until a global agreement is reached on ending the secrecy of banks and tax havens, there should be the encouragement of data leakage regarding these entities as in the case of Panama, British Virgin Islands, HSBC and LGT banks. Most data on people responsible for international wrongdoing that has been revealed in the last decade has been stolen data from banks and financial institutions.

Technology-related Aspects

Technology can help in solving the problem of the black economy provided the human element is honest. However, technology has also led to the emergence of new problems by creating new avenues of illegality— today, there is data theft from banks, the hacking of accounts, hacking of ATMs, phishing, etc. These need to be plugged by thinking ahead.

LONG TERM

Political Change Needed

There is need for the creation of genuine political will through public action to initiate change; this will lead to the cleaning up of elections and result in political party reform. Unfortunately, this is not going to happen automatically nor by the parties' own accord.

One way to bring about the accountability of politicians is to make them face elections. I have been in favour of half of the legislators facing elections every two and a half years so that the government can potentially change and will have to show to the public that it has delivered what it had promised. To make representation effective, there has to be a bottom-up approach. Leaders have to rise from the grassroots and not drop from the skies in helicopters as is the case at present. They should have served the people through grassroots activity and representation at the primary level (local bodies) before they can stand for any election at the higher levels. This way they will get to better understand the problems of the people and would have a good idea of their constituency. Similarly, they should not be allowed to stand from wherever they like and should have served a term in that constituency. Even this provision may not be enough for better representation since it could also be misused by the politicians.

A major reform required is that political parties function democratically. There is need for internal democracy. Many of today's leaders come up without serving the people and take over parties. Parties and constituencies are often passed on by political leaders to relatives like property. Such leaders are often contemptuous of the people and represent mostly the interest of society's upper crust.

Electoral reform is required so that genuine representatives of the people (i.e. those who are not purchasable by vested interests) enter the legislature. State funding of elections will not help since it only gives additional funds to the corrupt. Election expenses are often ten times the allowed limit and a bulk of the expenditure is on illegal activities and raised from illegal sources. State funding will not help/cannot be used to clean this up.

Citizens' groups which can present an independent record of the performance of the candidates before elections will help make voters better informed. Finally, exercising one's vote should not merely mean going to the polling booth on election day. A politically alert public— which votes consciously in the national interest, and not along caste and communal lines—is needed. Audit of accounts of political parties is suggested but accounts are easily manipulated. Businesses have demonstrated that they can hide their incomes in a variety of ways in spite of mandatory audit. The same technique can be adopted by the political parties. Audit will truly work only if transparency can be enforced in the functioning of the parties and their leadership.

One of the problems to be resolved is the role of political funding by big businesses. This is usually hidden from the public gaze. It leads to crony capitalism. This backdoor funding needs to be checked. The only way it can be curbed is via proper representation. If a politician has adequately served the people she/he would not need a lot of money for elections. Money is only needed to purchase vote banks, hire workers, and so on. A genuine leader of the people will not need to resort to such tactics.

Consensus on policies among political groups is crucial since that would reduce the need among parties for underhand dealing to represent the interest of the vested interests who control them. Competitive politics would also decline. Such a consensus has to be based on a bottom-up approach. If this happens, sectional interests will understand that their group interest can be only achieved via the collectivity rather than through sectional and sectarian policies. This would require the implementation of policies based on 'last person first' and would ensure that policies for the poor are effectively implemented, otherwise political conflict will continue.

Reform of the Corporates

Accountability of corporates means accountability to the shareholders and society at large. This is only possible if the board of governors and company auditors are accountable. There have to be independent directors on the boards of the companies to serve as public watchdogs. Such directors should be chosen from outside the triad. The members of the triad belong to the same class and have sympathy with the manipulations indulged in by businesses since they are also somewhere associated with such actions (this was the case with Satyam where the board of directors did not play the role expected of them). Directors should be made to pay for the wrong actions of companies they are associated with and to whom they are supposed to provide leadership. Chartered accountants have to be made accountable through fines if accounts are found to have been falsified.

Role of Movements

Political change is only possible with a change in the consciousness of the public. This requires the fostering of social movements for change. Such movements also make the public more aware of its rights. People's movements can be an effective check on politicians. It is argued that honest individuals are important. The issue is whether such people can change the system which causes the black economy to grow. An Arun Bhatia or a Khemka or a Seshan have done much good to the system even though they are from the executive. However, in any absolute sense, they have achieved little compared to what is needed.

What is needed therefore is a combination of large-scale movements by the people which will force change upon the political class and change that is initiated within the system by members of the executive. Only then will it be possible to dismantle the black economy.

CONCLUSION

In conclusion, I hope this book has succeeded in demystifying the black economy to some extent. It is a subject on which there is a lot of confusion and little understanding where most people, even economists and policy wonks, are concerned. Adding to the confusion is the fact that various governments have put their own spin on the black economy, either denying its existence or misrepresenting its causes and effects. As argued, dozens of committees and commissions have been set up to analyse the problem, but they have only looked at it from a partial or sectoral perspective. Thus, they have not been able to give an overview which is very much needed to understand the way in which it should be tackled.

The problem begins with the definition of the black economy. Even the term 'black economy' is racially loaded and inappropriate. It implies that black is bad while white is good. The problems multiply from that point onwards. We have seen how various definitions fall short of correctly describing the phenomenon. We have also seen what the difficulties are in measuring it. Most importantly, we have seen that there is no magic wand to solve the problem. That is because the heart of the problem is political and the political class and governments are an integral part of the reasons the black economy exists. Consequently, there is no attempt to seriously reform the system. Unsurprisingly, whichever party is in power at any given time makes no more than cosmetic changes to the system that brought it to power.

The only way in which the black economy can be successfully tackled is if successive governments show the political will to act. This will often mean they will have to act against their own supporters (especially financial backers), and their own party men so it will require men and women of vision to act with determination over the long term to thoroughly overhaul the system. For any long-term measure to succeed, besides the political will to root out the problem, a change in social consciousness is required—so that any systematic solution becomes a permanent one. This sort of change will require social movements all over the country. NGOs can create and strengthen movements to bring about this change. The last time we witnessed this sort of positive force for change was during the national movement. We will need to recapture that sort of spirit and commitment if we are to eliminate a problem that is endemic and flourishes because there is no concerted effort to get rid of it. Not that all the NGOs have done good work but there are many that have done a great job to help the people they work with. These movements need to get together and create a wider consciousness among society as a whole.

Movements can also help overcome the colonial disruption of our consciousness which has led to the persistence of feudal attitudes which weakens democracy. These are the very factors that reinforce and propel the black economy in India. This disruption also weakens the consciousness of the people and makes them accept their place in life as it is. Critically, the feudal consciousness of the ruling elite needs to be changed if the black economy is to be controlled.

It has been shown in this book that the black economy underlies the major socio-political and economic problems faced by India. It is the cause of macroeconomic problems like fiscal crises, inflation and BOP difficulties. Micro problems and sectoral problems of the economy, like poor and inadequate education, health and infrastructure are also linked to the black economy. It raises costs everywhere—leading to inefficiency everywhere. It weakens democracy. If not checked, India's growth story can become a thing of the past. Further, I have argued that it is not the inadequacy of laws that is at the root of the problem but their implementation that is the issue.

Simply put, the black economy has affected the social, political, economic and cultural life of India. It is in the nation's enlightened self-interest to curb it. In recent times, new political parties and social organizations have emerged to take up the issues of the people. We need more of them working in concert to make a dent in the problem. The fight against the black economy is nothing less than a fight to rebuild Indian society—to make it a more civilized, decent, democratic, and socially just society. It is a battle to usher in a society in which institutions, governments and the powerful become truly accountable. If the battle is won, it will be a game changer and we will have a country and a society that we can truly celebrate. The task is not easy but has the task of nation building ever been easy?

ACKNOWLEDGEMENTS

....~..

I was persuaded to write this book by David Davidar after he read an interview I had given to *Caravan* magazine about demonetization. I agreed since I thought it would be a good time to further the debate on the all-important but largely ignored topic of the black economy (especially as Modi's demonetization had been announced on the basis of the incorrect premise that the black economy was synonymous with cash).

Since I already had a lot of published and unpublished material, I felt that I could quickly write a book that would be analytical and yet not technical so that it would be accessible to the lay reader. The ideas that inform the book were first aired at the Nanda Memorial Lecture I delivered at Punjab University, Chandigarh, in November 2015. I have used some material from my articles in the *Indian Express, Mainstream* and the book *Transnational Organized Crime*. Chapter V is based on my talk at Yale University in November 2016.

113

I must thank David and Simar Puneet for rapidly editing the manuscript and Aienla Ozukum and her team at Aleph for handling the drafts and production-related assistance.

Arun Kumar
New Delhi
January 2017

APPENDIX

.................................~.................................

WAYS OF MEASURING THE SIZE OF THE BLACK ECONOMY

The aggregate size of the black economy is given relative to that of the white economy—as a percentage of the declared (white) GDP. Its separate components, like the black incomes earned in education, the legal profession and so on, are given in absolute numbers. The methods used are called trace methods since one looks for traces of the black economy in the visible white economy.

As mentioned in the book the four methods, broadly speaking, used to measure the size of the black economy are the survey approach, the input-output method, the monetarist approach and the fiscal approach. Let us look at each of these in turn.

SURVEY APPROACH

As the name suggests, this method depends on carrying out surveys. This is a good method, provided people report data honestly. If not, it is futile. In some countries, people feel it is their duty to report data correctly, but in India many people try to hide the facts either because they are confused and do not understand what is being asked of them or because they are trying to mislead the authorities for their own benefit.

In 1983, while conducting a survey in the sugarcane growing areas of Maharashtra, I asked the farmers to tell me what their income was. I soon realized that they only thought of cash revenue as income but anything in kind was not considered to be a part of their income. The poor among them thought that if they reported a lower income they could get government benefits. My experience was not unique; it is therefore easy to see why surveys often throw up bad data. For example, some consumption surveys show that even the poor consume expensive consumer goods. Given the income they declare it would be unlikely they could afford these items. The only explanation is that these people are under reporting incomes.

Accurate income surveys could provide a realistic estimate of the true income in the economy. By comparing this total with what the official agencies estimate, one could get a measure of the size of the black economy. During Indira Gandhi's Emergency in 1976, when most freedoms were suspended, the National Council of Applied and Economic Research (NCAER) conducted a survey of incomes on the assumption that due to the fear factor people would report them more accurately. But the figures that the survey threw up turned out to be 45 per cent less than the official figure of GDP. The implication is that not only did people not report their black incomes, they did not even fully report their white incomes. So, surveys can be rather unreliable.

The National Sample Survey Organization (NSSO) does surveys of consumption by asking a large sample of people for their monthly consumption over the year in question. This is used to estimate the distribution and the total consumption in the economy. Can this be used to estimate the size of the black economy? Not really. As incomes rise, consumption becomes a smaller and smaller part of one's income; savings and investment become more and more important. Hence, the better-off sections who generate black incomes are precisely the ones for whom consumption is not a good proxy for their incomes. Consequently, apart from other lacunae relating to biases in the sample, this method cannot estimate the black incomes generated.

INPUT-OUTPUT METHOD

This method is based on the notion that nothing can be produced without an input. This is a law not just of economics but is the foundational law of thermodynamics. The idea is that if we know how much input is required to produce an output—called the input-output ratio— we should be able to work out the aggregate output in the economy. When this is compared to the declared output it gives the estimate of the output not declared and which generates the black incomes.

One can use energy or labour as an input since all production requires both these inputs. The input-output ratio is technologically defined. Gupta and Mehta (1981), used energy as an input along with the technological ratio giving the amount of energy required to produce one unit of output (called energy intensity of production) to estimate the size of the black economy. However, as often happens in economics, what seems to be obvious and simple turns out to be horrendously complex to estimate.

The economy is very complex so the amount of energy required in each sector to produce a unit of output is vastly different. The energy required for steel, for instance, will be different from the energy required in agriculture to that used by a teacher to teach. Further, as time goes by, efficiency has improved. Cars may give three times the mileage from a litre of petrol than was the case fifty years back. A mobile phone does far more than a mainframe computer used to do in the 1960s with a power consumption that may be thousands of times less.

The form of energy has also changed over time. Earlier people used coal, cow dung and bio-mass. This has been largely replaced by electricity, diesel and gas. For irrigation and ploughing one used bullocks but now one uses diesel pumps and tractors. With all these technical changes, the efficiency of use of energy has changed. All this is hard to factor in for an entire economy. Thus, this method may work for an industry but not for an entire nation's economy. There are other technical lacunae with this method so it is hardly used. The NIPFP used it to estimate the black income generation in the sugar industry in 1960s and 70s.

MONETARIST APPROACH

This method is based on the idea that money is needed to circulate all transactions and incomes in an economy. Since all money supply in an economy depends on the central bank (in our case, the Reserve Bank of India) we are able to define it fairly well. Globally, this method is the most widely used. However, in India, as we have seen, the method used the most is the fiscal approach.

Money is needed to circulate both black and the white incomes; after all there is no colour on notes which denotes that some will circulate the black economy and others the white economy.

If we can figure out, using statistical techniques, how much money supply circulates the white economy then the balance can be attributed to the existence of the black economy. Using some simple formulae, this should yield the size of the black economy.

However, as stated earlier, what appears to be simple in economics is often hard to tackle due to data and conceptual problems. The segregation of money between the black and white economy is hard or impossible. Usually the assumption is that some variables (such as the tax variable) may be used to do this. But if we knew what the relationship between tax and black income generation is then we could directly use it and would not have to use the monetarist method.

As we know, there are a lot of deficiencies in the quality of the data available. So the use of the statistical techniques in the case of the monetarist approach turns out to be incorrect. The same problem occurs when the input-output method is used, since the ratio is distorted by the black economy. Further, these are aggregative methods and do not take into account sectoral differences. For instance, as I have explained earlier, agriculture does not generate black incomes but it uses money to circulate incomes. How to account for this is tricky. Similarly, most of the informal sector does not generate black incomes so this sector also needs to be separately dealt with. Finally, the financial sector generates a huge amount of transactions for small incomes. But the monetarist method is not able to deal with all these differences.

Under this approach a sophisticated method called MIMIC has been devised and used to estimate the size of the black economy for a large number of countries. It recognizes that the black economy is an unobserved variable which has an impact on various other variables in the system and they can be measured. Also, the black economy is affected by many other variables called input variables. Thus, using both these sets of variables for which data is available and applying esoteric statistical techniques, the size of the black economy is estimated.

The problem is that it uses the same variables for all the countries whereas each country has its own specificity which needs to be taken into account. Some may have to deal with a terrorist movement which engages in the smuggling of drugs and arms such as in Sri Lanka when the LTTE was a major force. Some may have to cope with a strong network of narcotic drug cartels (like

Colombia). Others might need to factor in the presence of a corrupt dictatorship (like Egypt). Yet others might have a weak democracy where accountability is missing and the flouting of rules is widespread. Because of these factors one should analyse the black economy in each country specifically with its institutional details taken into account.

Importantly, as has been pointed out earlier, the black economy is different in advanced and developing countries. This dissimilarity must be taken into account and that is why the same method cannot be applied for all the economies. In developed countries, as I've mentioned, the black economy may largely comprise wage and salary incomes while in developing economies it emanates from property (not real estate) incomes. Further, while in the advanced economies black incomes are generated largely in the informal and illegal sectors, in the developing countries a bulk of the black incomes are generated in the formal and the legal sectors.

Since the monetarist method is unable to differentiate between the formal and informal sectors, it counts the part of the informal sector not accounted in the national income as black which is not correct for the Indian economy. Finally, the method is based on counting transactions that are not captured and as transactions are a large multiple of the incomes earned in the economy, it tends to give a high figure for the black economy. In brief, due to the above mentioned lacunae, the monetarist method and the MIMIC approach are not useful in the Indian context. A World Bank paper estimate of black incomes in India for 2010 is based on this method and is therefore not very useful. Similarly, the estimate by Gupta and Gupta for 1978 gives a high figure of 47 per cent but it is not a reliable estimate because of definitional reasons.

FISCAL APPROACH

As has already been mentioned, this method is definitionally the correct way to estimate the size of the black economy in India. Various estimates of the black economy in India using the fiscal approach are:

Year	Black economy as a percentage of GDP	Estimated by
1956	4.5	Kaldor (1956)
1970	7	Wanchoo Committee (1970)
1976-77	10.2	Chopra (own method) (1982)
1980-81 to '83	18 to 21	NIPFP (1985)

1980-81	15	Basu (1995)
1990-91	35	Kumar (1999)
1995-96	40	Kumar (1999)

I have used the above estimates to project to the recent period. The method is based on taking into account the main institutional factors in India. It recognizes that illegality is at the heart of the black income generation and this is taken to be represented by the level of crime per lakh of population. Similarly, it takes into account the fact that the bulk of black incomes are generated in the services sector of the economy and also that it is linked to over- and-under invoicing in foreign trade. Of course, there could be other factors but for the sake of simplicity these were the main factors that were taken into account.

As has been mentioned, according to this approach the size of the black economy today has increased to 62 per cent of GDP. This figure is not comparable to estimates from other methods, because of definitional issues and their lack of analytical clarity.

◆

One final point can be made about measuring the black economy. Transparency International annually brings out a Corruption Index that ranks various countries by their level of corruption in the public sector. The index goes from 0 to 100 with the most corrupt being at 100 and the least corrupt being at zero. In its 2015 report, India ranked 76 out of 168 countries for which data was given. It achieved a score of 38. This does not give the size of the black economy for a country but gives its relative standing in the world. Thus, if India reduces its level of corruption by the same amount as all the other countries, then its ranking does not change. If other countries do better than India, while India also reduces its level of corruption, India will slip and appear to be worse off, which is not the case in an absolute sense.

The major problem with these indices is that they are based on a survey of business managers who give their ranking and scores of the level of corruption that they have perceived in different countries. That is why it is called the 'Corruption Perceptions Index'. One of the deficiencies of this index is that it ignores black income generation in the private sector. It is also often the case that the data is based on a biased sample; it takes the opinion of business managers but does not take into account what the people of a country may face, especially in the non-corporate sectors. The corporate sector is powerful but rather small in most of the developing world and not representative of the rest of the people in a country. The kind of corruption the business managers may face is likely to be completely different to what others face. Hence, the Transparency International Index is not very useful for policy purposes.

SOME FINANCIAL AND ECONOMIC
TERMS USED IN THE TEXT

Balance of Payments (BoP)

It captures the record of all the economic transactions of citizens of a country with the economic entities of the rest of the world over the year. So, it refers to a nation's situation regarding its trade (what is imported into the country and what is exported from the country) of goods and services (called current account) and capital flows (called capital account and includes all the capital coming into the country and that going out of it) in relation to all other nations. So, there is a balance (surplus or deficit) on current account and another on capital account. The two together make up the overall balance. This last item represents broadly the change in the official reserves of the country. A surplus (deficit) would lead to a rise (fall) in the foreign exchange reserves of the country.

Base Erosion Profit Shifting (BEPS)

This refers to the MNCs taking their profits out of their country of origin to those countries/tax havens where the tax rates are low. This way they pay lower taxes on their profits in the country of their origin (thus 'profit shifting') and given that the tax base is lowered, it is called base erosion.

capital account convertibility

It refers to the possibility of taking one's capital and converting it to another currency so that it can be freely taken out of the country and brought back without any problems. It requires one's currency to be accepted internationally.

factor income

These are incomes that are generated in production. They can be wages or property incomes. Property incomes can be profits, rent interest or dividend.

fiscal deficit

This is the excess of expenditure by the government over its own resources. In other words, what the government borrows is not counted as its own resource.

hawala

This refers to a parallel banking channel which is outside the regulation of the central bank (RBI). It may be used to transfer funds both within and outside India.

income distribution

It gives the split of national income between profits and wages. It represents the skewedness of factor incomes in the economy.

incremental capital-output ratio

It is the ratio of change in the capital stock to the change in the output of the economy. It tells us how much capital is needed to produce one unit of output in the economy. It varies from sector to sector. So, it would be high in, say, the steel industry but low in traditional agriculture.

input-output ratio

It stands for how much input is needed to produce one unit of output. It depends on the technology in the economy and changes with time as technology changes.

investment multiplier

The investment multiplier is a relation between national income and the investment in the economy. It tells us how many times of the investment is the national income. This multiplier is the inverse of the savings rate in the economy.

layering

This is the process of taking illicit funds out of the economy via tax havens. Funds are transferred from a shell company in one tax haven to another, after which the shell company in the first tax haven is closed so that the track of fund movement is obliterated. It is like moving funds from one layer to another, hence the term 'layering'. Funds may be transferred through up to six tax havens until they reach the ultimate destination (say, Switzerland).

license-permit-quota raj
It refers to the elaborate system of licences, regulations and accompanying red tape. Entrepreneurs had to deal with it if they wanted to set up and run businesses in India between 1947 and 1990.

Lokpal
This is the name for the ombudsman or an anti-corruption authority. He would head an anti-corruption body which could look at the corruption of Members of Parliament and employees of government. A bill was passed in December 2013 to set up this institution.

marketization
This term implies the penetration of market principles/thinking into all institutions of society. It leads to greater play of the markets in the economy by reducing government intervention. Further, there is the greater play of principles on which markets operate, namely 'dollar vote', 'more is better', 'consumer sovereignty', 'rational individual' and so on, in society.

middle-income country
These are countries that are listed between the low-income and high-income countries. The World Bank defined these in 2015 (using the World Bank Atlas method) as having a per capita income between $1,026 and $12,475. This is a wide range of incomes so is a rather diverse set of countries.

national income/GDP
It is the total income earned by all the nationals of a country from all the economic activities carried out in a year. The economy is made up of the primary, secondary and tertiary sectors. These are further broken down into nine major sectors. The income contribution from each of these sectors is added up to get the total national income.

Since an individual can earn a property income or a wage income the national income is made up of the sum of these two.

non-performing assets (NPA)
Refers to the loans given out by banks on which repayment is due. Repayment could be of capital or the interest due. When those borrowers face financial difficulties, they are unable to pay the banks making them the NPAs of the banks. The idea is that the bank's assets are not giving the return they are supposed to give.

opportunity cost
When one makes a choice between several available alternatives then it is the loss that may be incurred as compared to the other alternatives. If one takes out capital and consumes it then one misses out on the interest that one could have earned on it by investing it. That is the opportunity cost.

per capita income
The income that each citizen would earn if the entire national income is divided equally between all citizens.

potential rate of growth
The rate of growth which could be achieved if the black economy is eliminated so that the productivity of investment becomes higher and the level of investment rises.

presumptive tax
This is a tax collected on the basis of some indicators and not on the actual reported income. So, if a doctor is seen to have a practice in a posh market and has a clinic which is of a certain size then there would be a presumption of a certain income and tax would be collected on that basis. In the case of services it is difficult to say what fee is being charged. For professions like doctors, lawyers or teachers giving tuition, a presumptive tax could be used.

property income
Refers to incomes which accrue due to ownership of some form of capital. So, interest would be earned on financial capital, rent on building and land, profit on capital invested and dividend on ownership of shares.

revenue budget
The budget is made up of two parts—revenue and capital. The revenue part has all those items that have no link with the next year, like administrative expenditures, or subsidy payments, interest payment or tax collection. The capital part has a link with the next year like borrowing, on which an interest has to be paid next year, or an investment on which future income would be earned.

round tripping
The return of capital that was earlier illegally sent abroad.

transfer income
These are incomes that are generated during the transfer of assets, like the sale of real estate or shares in the secondary markets. Payment of bribes also falls in this category.

wholesale price index
It is the index of wholesale prices prevailing in the country. It is taken to represent the price level in the economy and the percentage change in it is taken to give the rate of inflation in the economy.

NOTES AND REFERENCES

.... ∼ ....

INTRODUCTION

xv **it has been shown that the black economy is a joint product**: F. A. Cowell, *Cheating the Government*, Cambridge, Massachusetts: MIT Press, 1990.

xvii **According to a study, the opportunity cost of the flight of capital for the Indian economy**: A. Kumar, and S. Chattopadhyay, 'Estimates of Illicit Financial Flows Pertaining to India', 1948 to 2012. Mimeo. Paper presented at the seminar on 'Black Economy in India, its Global Dimensions and Impact on Policies', organized by CESP, JNU and TJN, at JNU on 26 June 2015.

xix **While the biggest scam prior to 1990 was the Bofors Scam**: 'Key Players in Bofors Scandal', *India Today*, 28 April 2009.

xix **The largest was the Harshad Mehta-led Stock Market Scam of 1991-1992**: Arun Kumar, 'From Bofors to 2G, the same fate', *The Hindu*, 24 May 2013.

xix **In the first decade of this century, there was a flood of revelations**: Arun Kumar, *Indian Economy Since Independence: Persisting Colonial Disruption*, New Delhi: Vision Books, 2013.

I. WHAT IS THE BLACK ECONOMY?

4-5 That is why out of a population of almost 130 crore, only about 5.2 crore people are in the tax net: Arun Kumar, 'Curbing Black Economy: Not by Good Intentions Alone', *Economic & Political Weekly*. Vol. 51, Issue No. 36, 3 September 2016

15 the IT company reportedly had 13,000 fictitious employees on its rolls: 'Satyam has 13,000 ghost employees', *Business Standard*, 23 January 2009.

19-20 The debate between economists Paul Baran and Nicholas Kaldor is instructive: P. A. Baran, *The Political Economy of Growth*, Harmondsworth: Pelican Books, 1973.

21 Using the fiscal approach, the size of the black economy was estimated: White paper on 'Black Money', Ministry of Finance, Department of Revenue, Central Board of Direct Taxes, New Delhi, May 2012.

II. THE BLACK ECONOMY IN INDIA TODAY

24 'outlays [expenditures] do not necessarily: Sharad Joshi, *Hindu Business Line*, 7 September 2005.

25 According to a Pratham report, 50 per cent of schoolchildren in the fifth grade: Pratham Education Foundation Annual Report 2011-2012.

26 'digging holes and filling them: Arun Kumar, *The Black Economy in India*, New Delhi: Penguin, 1999.

29 black incomes comprise factor incomes which are property incomes that are not reported: Ibid.

30 It has been shown that wages are inflated to show higher costs and generate black incomes: Ibid; see also 'Black Economy, Underestimation of Employment and the Union Budget', *Economic & Political Weekly*, Vol. XLI No 30, 29 July 2006, pp. 3315-20.

30 **Since profits tend to be larger than the wages, the share of high incomes rises:** Arun Kumar, 'India's Black Economy: The Macroeconomic Implications', *South Asia: Journal of South Asian Studies,* Vol. 28 No.2, August 2005, pp. 249-263.

30 **It has also been shown that the rate of investment in the economy falls due to the black economy:** Kumar, *Black Economy in India.*

31 **The incremental capital-output ratio rises because of the inefficient use of capital due to the black economy:** Kumar, *South Asia: Journal of South Asian Studies,* August 2005.

33 **Consequently, the velocity of circulation…calculated with white economy data:** Arun Kumar, 'Impact of Black Economy on Fiscal and Monetary Aspects of the Indian Economy', Mimeo at the Round Table Discussion on Financial Reforms in India. Organized by the Academy of Third World Studies, Jamia Islamia and Mushashi Research Team, Japan, 7 March 2007.

34 **It is adversely affected due to various factors linked to the black economy:** See Arun Kumar, 'Illegal Flows in India's BOP Accounts: Its Components and Impact on the Economy' in B. Dasgupta (ed.), *External Dimensions of an Emerging Economy, India: Essays in Honour of Sunanda Sen,* London: Routledge, 2013, pp. 28-43.

35 **These illegal transactions are difficult to track and estimate due to:** Kumar, *Black Economy in India.*

36-37 **I estimated that the black economy was concentrated in the hands of:** Ibid.

37-38 **Another manifestation of such skewed income levels is that the savings propensity:** Kumar, *South Asia: Journal of South Asian Studies,* August 2005.

38 **A study from Kerala, between 1987 and 1996:** Nandraj, S., et al, Private Health Sector in India: Review and Annotated Bibliography, Mumbai: CEHAT, 2001.

41 **As has been pointed out in a recent study, if one were to take**

into account illegal activities: A. Kumar and S. Chattopadhyay, 'Estimates of Illicit Financial Flows Pertaining to India, 1948 to 2012'. Mimeo. Paper presented at the Seminar on 'Black Economy in India, its Global Dimensions and Impact on Policies' organized by CESP, JNU and TJN, at JNU on 26 June 2015.

41 **These flows take place in many ways but very importantly through shell companies set up in tax havens:** R. Palan, R. Murphy, and C. Chavagneux, *Tax Havens: How Globalization Really Works*, Ithaca and London: Cornell University, 2011.

III. ORIGINS AND GROWTH

49 **The Government of India report of 1956 argued for the need to keep the black economy in check:** *Direct Tax Reform: Report of a Survey* (Chairperson: Kaldor), Government of India, 1956.

50 **A strategy of import substitution was adopted to boost industry and high customs duties were introduced:** A more detailed discussion of these developments is in Kumar, *Indian Economy Since Independence*.

50 **In 1944, representatives of Indian big business drew up a plan of industrialization:** Sir P. Thakurdas and others, *A Plan of Economic Development for India*, London: Penguin, 1944.

53 **During the period that its import was banned (until 1992):** A. Sarma, A. Vasudevan, K. Kanagasabapathy, M. Narayan and M. Roy, 'Gold Mobilisation as an Instrument of External Adjustment: A Discussion Paper', Development Research Group, Department of Economic Analysis and Policy, Reserve Bank of India. Mumbai, 1992.

53 **The amount of gold inflow increased to 900 tons by 1998:** Kumar, *Black Economy in India*.

55 **the rise in this ratio is not due to a reduction of the black economy through improved compliance with the tax regime:**

'Macro Overview', Alternative Survey Group (ed.), *Alternative Economic Survey, India 2006-07: Pampering Corporates, Pauperizing Masses*, New Delhi: Daanish Books, 2007, pp. 37-39.

IV. WHAT FUELS THE BLACK ECONOMY?

62-63   A 2007 Alternative Economic Survey article showed that the rise in the direct tax: Ibid.

63   A 2016 *Economic and Political Weekly* article shows that even though the number of people in the direct tax net has risen to 52 million: Arun Kumar, 'Curbing Black Economy: Not by Good Intentions Alone'.

63   A National Institute of Public Finance and Policy (NIPFP) 1985 publication showed that in the case of the sugar industry: *Aspects of Black Economy in India*, New Delhi: NIPFP, 1985.

73   An amnesty was given to smugglers in 1983: B. V. Kumar, *The Darker Side of Black Money: An Insight Into the World of Financial Secrecy & Tax Havens*, New Delhi: Konark Publishers, 2011.

74   they have been paying the local press per column centimetre for positive coverage: Kumar, *Black Economy in India*.

V. REMEDIES

77   Some of these steps have not only not helped curb the menace but have in fact fuelled it: Ibid.

78   As discussed earlier, the underlying cause is the triad, which implies: See F. A. Cowell, *Cheating the Government*, MIT Press, Cambridge, Massachusetts, 1990 and 'The Chequered Economy in Black and White', book review of Kamal Nayan Kabra's book, *The Black Economy in India: Problems and Policies*, in *Economic*

& Political Weekly, Vol. 20 No. 13, 30 March 1985.

86 **According to the Pew Research Centre, in 2015, only 22 per cent of adults in India had access to the internet:** Jacob Poushter, 'Smartphone Ownership and Internet Usage Continues to Climb in Emerging Economies', www.pewglobal. org, 22 February 2016.

86 **Only 17 per cent of Indians have access to smart phones and consequently to mobile phone banking:** Ibid. Also see Venkat Ananth, 'Only 17% Indians own smartphones: survey', *LiveMint*, 24 February 2016.

86 **In a population of 1.3 billion and counting, there are 24.5 million credit cards and 661.8 million debit cards:** Itika Sharma Punit, 'After demonetisation dream run, Paytm is paying a price for its sudden stardom', *Scroll.in*, 25 December 2016.

91-92 **It was open from 1 June to 30 September 2016, during which time:** 'Black money haul: Rs 65,250 crore disclosed through Income Declaration Scheme', *Economic Times*, 1 October 2016.

93 **However, it has led to collateral damage by providing the route for round tripping from Mauritius:** Paranjoy Guha Thakurta, 'Plugging the Mauritius Loophole', *rediff.com*, 8 June 2002. http://www.rediff.com/money/2002/jun/08paran. html. Accessed on 17 August 2016.

93 **data suggest that illicit flows from the country have increased since 1991:** Arun Kumar, 'Measuring Illegal Flows from the Indian Economy: Some Methodological Issues', *Economic & Political Weekly*, Vol. XLVII No. 39. 29 September 2012, pp. 71-74.

98 **In a document brought out in 1994, I suggested many changes:** Proposals for a Citizens' Union Budget for the Nation for 1994-1995. An Alternative to the Fund-Bank Dictated Union Budget for 1994-1995. Presented to the Citizens' Committee on 12 February 1994 at Gandhi Peace Foundation, New Delhi. Prepared for the Preparatory Committee for Alternative

Economic Policies.

CONCLUSION

APPENDIX

SELECT BIBLIOGRAPHY

Acharya, Shankar N. and Associates with Contributions by Chelliah, R. J., *Aspects of the Black Economy*, New Delhi: National Institute of Public Finance and Policy (NIPFP), 1985.

Baran, Paul A., *The Political Economy of Growth*, Harmondsworth: Pelican Books Ltd., 1973.

Basu, S., 'Re-estimation of the Size of the Black Income in India in the Eighties: A Reappraisal of the NIPFP Estimation', unpublished MPhil Dissertation submitted to Centre for Economic Studies and Planning, School of Social Sciences, New Delhi: Jawaharlal Nehru University, 1995.

'Black Money: White Paper', New Delhi: Government of India, Ministry of Finance, Department of Revenue, Central Board of Direct Taxes, 2012.

Boyce, James K. and Rishi, Meenakshi, 'The Hidden Balance of Payments: Capital Flight and Trade Misinvoicing in India, 1971-1986', *Economic & Political Weekly, Volume. 25, No. 30*, 28 July 1990.

Chattopadhyay, S., 'Measuring the Size of the Underground Economy: A Critique of the MIMIC Approach', *Bharatiya Samajik Chintan*, Indian Social Science Academy, pp. 57-68, April-June, 2005.

Chopra, O. P., 'Unaccounted Income: Some Estimates', *Economic & Political Weekly, Volume. 17, No. 17/18*, pp. 739-744, 24 April 1982.

Cowell, F. A., *Cheating the Government: The Economics of Evasion*, Cambridge, Massachusetts: MIT Press, 1990.

'Direct Taxes Enquiry Report', *Wanchoo Committee Report*, New Delhi: Government of India, Ministry of Finance, 1971.

Gupta, Poonam, and Gupta, Sanjeev, 'Estimates of the Unreported Economy in India', *Economic & Political Weekly*, 16 January 1982.

Gupta, Suraj B., *Black Income in India*, New Delhi: Sage Publications, 1992.

Gupta, S. and Mehta, R., 'An Estimate of Underreported National Income', *Journal of Income and Wealth, Volume. 5, No. 2*, July 1981.

'Income Tax Department Time Series Data Financial Year 2000-01 to 2014-15', New Delhi: Government of India. Accessed on 18 August 2016. http://www.incometaxindia.gov.in/Documents/Time-Series-Data-Final.pdf.

Kaldor, N., 'Indian Tax Reform: Report of a Survey', New Delhi: Government of India, Ministry of Finance, 1956.

Kar, Dev, 'The Drivers and Dynamics of Illicit Financial Flows from India: 1948-2008', *Global Financial Integrity*, 17 November 2010. http://india.gfip.org.

Kumar, Arun, 'The Chequered Economy in Black and White', *Economic & Political Weekly, Volume. 20, No. 13*, 30 March 1985.

———, *The Black Economy of India*, New Delhi: Penguin Books, 1999.

———, 'India's Black Economy: The Macroeconomic Implications', *South Asia: Journal of South Asian Studies, Volume. 28, No. 2*, pp. 249-263, August 2005.

———, 'Fiscal Policies, Black Economy and Challenge of Education in India', in Arora, D., *Social Sector Development: From Outlays to Outcomes*. New Delhi: IIPA and Daanish Books, 2005, pp. 110-116.

———, 'Black Economy, Under Estimation of Employment and the Union Budget', *Economic & Political Weekly, Volume. XLI, No. 30*, pp. 3315-3320, 29 July 2006.

———, 'Macro Overview', Alternative Survey Group (ed.),

Alternative Economic Survey, India 2006-07: Pampering Corporates, Pauperizing Masses, pp. 37-39, New Delhi: Daanish Books, 2007.

————, 'Measuring Illegal Outflows from the Indian Economy', *Economic & Political Weekly, Volume. 47, No. 39*, pp. 71-74, 29 September 2012.

————, *Indian Economy Since Independence: Persisting Colonial Disruption*, New Delhi: Vision Books, 2013.

————, 'Black Economy in India and Transnational Organized Crime: Undermining Democracy', Stiftung, Heinrich Böll and Schönenberg, Regine (eds.), *Transnational Organized Crime: Analyses of a Global Challenge to Democracy*, Berlin: Transcript and *Heinrich Böll Foundation*, pp. 115-126, 2013.

————, 'Illegal Flows in India's BOP Accounts: Their Components and Impact on the Economy', Byasdeb Dasgupta (ed.), *External Dimension of an Emerging Economy, India: Essays in Honour of Sunanda Sen*, pp. 28-43, London: Routledge, 2013.

————, 'Curbing Black Economy: Not by Good Intentions Alone', *Economic & Political Weekly,* Vol. 51, Issue No. 36, 03 Sep, 2016

————, 'Estimation of the Size of the Black Economy in India, 1996–2012', *Economic & Political Weekly, Volume. 51, No. 48*, pp. 36–42, 26 November 2016.

Palan, Ronen, Murphy, Richard and Chavagneux, Christian, *Tax Havens: How Globalization Really Works*, Ithaca: Cornell University Press, 2010.

Reserve Bank of India, *Reports of the Committee to Enquire into Securities Transactions of Banks and Financial Institution: Janakiraman Committee Appointed by the Reserve Bank of India*, Bombay: Reserve Bank of India, 1993.

Sarma, Atul, Vasudevan, A., Kanagasabapathy, K., Naryan, M. and Roy, M., 'Gold Mobilisation as an Instrument of External Adjustment: A Discussion Paper', Development Research Group, Department of Economic Analysis and Policy, Bombay: Reserve Bank of India, 1992.

Schneider, Friedrich, Andreas Buehn and Claudio E. Montenegro.

2010. 'Shadow Economies All over the World: New Estimates for 162 Countries from 1999 to 2007'. Mimeo. The World Bank, Policy Research Working Paper 5356

Transparency International, 2015. Accessed on 23 December 2016. http://www.transparency.org/cpi2015.

INDEX

143

www.ingramcontent.com/pod-product-compliance
Lightning Source LLC
Chambersburg PA
CBHW031359180326
41458CB00043B/6545/J